CLONING GRAMEEN BANK

Very best wishes,

Helen Todd

Cloning Grameen Bank

Replicating a Poverty Reduction Model in India, Nepal and Vietnam

Edited by HELEN TODD

IT PUBLICATIONS 1996

Intermediate Technology Publications Ltd,
103-105 Southampton Row, London WC1B 4HH, UK

© Cashpor Technical Services Sdn. Bhd. 1996

A CIP record for this book is available from the British Library

ISBN 1 85339 390 8

Typeset by Dorwyn Ltd, Rowlands Castle, Hants
Printed in the UK by BPC Exeter

Contents

Figures

Acknowledgments

THIS BOOK SHOULD have been four reports slapped between two covers and delivered to APDC as part of a contract to evaluate four Grameen Bank replications which APDC jointly funded with the Grameen Trust. There are two reasons why it grew into a book. First, the human beings involved, the borrowers, the field staff and the project leaders, refused to be left out of the story, and demand a fuller treatment than a project evaluation could encompass. Second, there is little published information available about replications of the Grameen Bank methodology in Asia, and almost nothing on the third generation projects featured here. Given the amount of rhetoric now being heard on the model, it seems important to ground the dialogue in the processes and problems faced in actual attempts at replication and the factors involved in moving towards greater outreach and sustainability.

The transition from report to book received the full encouragement of Dr Mike Getubig of APDC. APDC funded the editor's field visits to the projects and was understanding about the extra time involved in preparing the book. We also gratefully acknowledge the Government of Canada, who through the Canadian Cooperation Support Office in Malaysia, provided the funding needed to rework the material into a manuscript on the experiences of these four projects and the lessons learned for the replication process.

Note
The units of measurement in the text are those which seemed appropriate when describing individual conditions. Conversions are as follows:

1 acre	=	0.405 hecatares
1 hectare	=	2.471 acres
1 mile	=	1.609 kilometres
1 kilometre	=	0.6214 miles

Introduction

A CENTRAL BANKER. An appropriate-technology NGO organizer. A professor of international relations. A top-level communist official. What could these four people possibly have in common?

All of them, in various ways, were concerned with poverty in their own countries and were disillusioned and frustrated with the weapons they were using to fight it. Dr H.D. Pant, Deputy Governor of the Nepal Rastra (Central) Bank spent more than a decade trying to regulate commercial banks into lending to the poor, with little success. Mr Udaia Kumar, Executive Secretary of a Indian NGO in Hyderabad transferring innovative technologies to the village, worked for years organizing skills training for people who had no capital to use them. Professor Jayanta Kumar Ray, the author of a book on the Grameen Bank,[1] raged quietly against the failure of the Marxist government in West Bengal to relieve the desperate poverty of the rural masses in whose name they governed. Mdm Do Thi Tan built a career in the 11 million member Women's Union in Vietnam organizing conventional health and child care programmes for women, but increasingly worried how economic liberalization was leaving poor rural women behind.

All were looking for another method to break the poor out of the iron structures that kept them poor. Between 1985 and 1991 each one of them travelled to Bangladesh and took a close look at the Grameen Bank. They saw an organization which was delivering financial services to hundreds of thousands of families through a methodology which seemed to work. It targeted poor women exclusively; it was simple, accessible and honest; it used both group solidarity and individual enterprise to boost the incomes and asset base of poor families. Dr Pant, Mr Udaia, Professor Ray and Mdm Tan each separately decided that this was a model of great promise if only they could import it and adapt it to their own national contexts.

In the early 1990s several institutions came together to make possible the import of this successful Grameen Bank model into other countries in Asia. Grameen Bank, with funding from GTZ in Germany, formalized the increasing stream of people coming to look at the way the Bank worked, by beginning a series of 'International Grameen Dialogues'. These invited participants from all over the world to spend a week in a Grameen Bank branch following staff on their work rounds and talking to borrowers. Participants would then reassemble in Dhaka to debate what they had seen and relate it to their own national contexts. This exposure to Grameen banking, experienced by Mr Udaia and Mdm. Tan during 1991, resulted in a number of proposals from participants to create replicas or adaptations of the Grameen Bank in other countries.

Well before this, however, there were already eight replications at various stages of development in Asia, three of them midwifed by a programme pioneered by the Asia Pacific Development Centre (APDC), an intergovernmental body based in Kuala Lumpur, Malaysia. In 1985, Professor David Gibbons and Associate Professor Sukor Kasim, poverty researchers at the University Science Malaysia, spent three weeks with the Grameen Bank to see if its methods could be used to reach the hard-core poor in rural peninsular Malaysia. When they decided to pilot test it, they approached APDC for operating funds. Initially they were told, as replicators in many countries would continue to be told over the next decade: 'This is not the kind of thing we do.'

But APDC happened to have a Malaysian director at that time, Dr Mohd. Shahari, who was interested in the idea. APDC's Employment and Rural Development Section, under Dr Mike Getubig, put up a paper to its funding agency, UNDP. One of UNDP's consultants examined it. It is simplistic, he said, for a couple of academics to think they can take a successful programme in one country and parachute it into a completely different socioeconomic context. It will not work. APDC should not fund it, he advised. But Dr Shahari decided to stick his neck out. Gibbons and Sukor were already by this time working in the paddy fields of coastal Selangor, forming their first credit groups. Gibbons wrote a paper entitled: *So Far, So Good*, which Dr Shahari fired off to the consultant. Dr Getubig set up the 'Grameen Bank Replication Programme', with Project Ikhtiar as its only child, and Gibbons and Sukor got the funds they needed to continue.[2] This two year pilot proved that the GB methodology *did* work in the very different context of rural Malaysia; Project Ikhtiar was institutionalized into Amanah Ikhtiar Malaysia (AIM) in 1987 and over the next four years, rapidly expanded to 34 branches that would eventually enrol nearly half of the hard-core poor in Peninsular Malaysia.

For APDC this success was equally significant. Their main funder, the UNDP, commented in an evaluation of the entire APDC work programme, that 'in terms of promoting development, the only project to have a *visible* impact was the Grameen Bank replication project.' Encouraged, Dr Getubig moved to extend the replication programme, and further pilot test the Grameen Bank model in other Asian contexts. Between 1988 and 1991 APDC funded Ahon Sa Hirap (ASHI) in the Philippines and Karya Usaha Mandiri (KUM) in Indonesia, both, like Project Ikhtiar, action-research projects.

In the meantime, others were trying out the Grameen model on their own. The AIM example encouraged IDS, a state government think-tank in Sabah, East

Malaysia, to begin Usahamaju there. Several NGOs in the Philippines sent their leaders to Grameen Bank in Bangladesh, who returned to begin their own pilot programmes. In Sri Lanka, the country representative of Redd Barna, Andreas Fuglesang, who with Dale Chandler had written the first thorough description of the workings of the Grameen Bank,[3] added Savecred to Redd Barna's community development programme.

In October 1991, APDC called all of these actors to an awe-inspiring, rainswept mountain resort in Kundasang, Sabah for a seminar on Grameen Bank replication. The seven replicators complained bitterly to each other of the lack of funding to expand their pilot projects into full-scale credit programmes. One visit to Grameen Bank was not enough to learn the methodology, they said. They needed to know a lot more so that they could in turn better train their field staff. They agreed that these three days talking to other replicators gave an immense boost to both their knowledge and their confidence. We want more dialogues like this one, they said. Before they left for home, the seven project heads, Dr Getubig, and Mr. Khalid Shams, the Deputy Managing Director of the Grameen Bank, resolved to form a network of hands-on Grameen Bank replicators who would share experiences, conduct training and technical assistance between themselves and try to mobilize funds for members. This was the beginning of CASHPOR — Credit and Savings for the Hard-Core Poor — and Dr Mike Getubig from APDC became its first Executive Secretary.

But the surge of interest in Grameen-style credit was not confined to Asia. The Grameen Bank itself was being bombarded by NGOs, academics, donors and government agencies who wanted to try Grameen in different parts of the world. In 1992, Grameen Bank set up a foundation called Grameen Trust to vet some of the applications coming out of the International Grameen Dialogues and channel funds (initially, also coming from GTZ in Germany) to help them get started. So when APDC began considering Phase Three of its Grameen Bank Replication Programme, another funder, Grameen Trust (GT), was now in the field. Since APDC had enough money to fund only two new replications, and there were four promising candidates identified, GT and APDC decided to fund all four jointly and to work together to train their staff and monitor their progress.

The Issue is Viability

The objectives of Phase Three were shaped by the impatience of the three men who sat in the planning meeting. Dr Getubig of APDC, Dr Muhammad Yunus, Grameen Bank MD, and Professor David Gibbons, MD of AIM, had seen enough 'pilot' projects successfully testing the replicability of the Grameen Bank methodology in a variety of contexts to think that any more tests were unnecessary. They felt that 'new replications should be started as the first phase of a programme that is expected to be ongoing and expanded so as to serve large numbers of poor households.'[4] They were looking for the kind of project which could take off to reach really large numbers and make a macro-impact on poverty.

This emphasis also grew from the disappointment they felt with the lack of growth in both KUM and ASHI after the modest targets of the pilot phase had been met. Dr Getubig commented:

> They did O.K., but they seemed doomed to stagnate because there was no real will or capacity to expand. So for phase three we were looking for organizations who were willing to go big and who worked in an environment with the poverty density so that they could. We didn't want showpiece projects, but those who could expand, become sustainable and make a difference. And we wanted the kind of leaders who could attract the funding required to do that. So the issue for phase three was not: Can you replicate it? The issue was: Can you make it viable?[5]

This meant that the pilot project had to think from the beginning in terms of institutionalising — creating the capacity in trained staff and efficient systems to expand into a full-scale programme delivering financial services to the poor. It also had to plan from its inception to make enough income to cover its costs as soon as possible, consistent with the overriding goal of meeting the credit and savings needs of its clients. The funding traumas of earlier projects, particularly those in the Philippines, had taught that planning for viability was vital — so that projects could win independence from donors, so that credibility could be established with local banks to get on-lending funds for expansion, so that the programme could be sustained for as long as its clients needed it.

The selection of the four projects for Phase Three was very much an outcome of the CASHPOR network and its close working relationship with the Grameen Bank. There was a strong feeling that APDC should be looking at the subcontinent, especially India, both because of its similarity to Bangladesh conditions and because it had the largest number of poor people in the world. Gibbons heard about Mr. Udaia Kumar of SHARE from Associate Professor Sukor Kasim of AIM, who shared a room with Udaia during an International Grameen Dialogue. 'He's really serious,' Sukor said. 'He never stops taking notes!' Gibbons visited Udaia at Hyderabad and went with him to several prospective project sites. Then Gibbons stopped in Calcutta and advised Professor Ray, who had attempted to establish a GB replication in 1988 but failed to get the state government's co-operation, that now was the chance to try again. Dr Getubig made an exploratory visit to Nepal with names given by the Grameen Bank and met Dr Pant and his colleagues in Nirdhan Nepal. Meanwhile, the founder of CARD, Mr Aristotle Alip, which initiated a Grameen-type credit programme in the Philippines in 1989 and was a CASHPOR member, became credit adviser to CIDSE in Vietnam in 1991. There he cultivated the leaders of the Women's Union, who were already exploring different models of delivering credit to women microentrepreneurs.

Yunus, Gibbons and Getubig were very excited about the prospect of a GB replication being tried in Vietnam. It was a transitional socialist economy; its people, because of war and the 20-year US ban on all international assistance, were very poor. But all three also had the idea of China hovering in their minds. As Gibbons put it: '[Tau Yew Mai's] significance in terms of the relevance and applicability of the GB approach in a socialist country undertaking market-oriented economic reforms, can hardly be overestimated.'[6]

India, Nepal and Vietnam all had very high densities of poverty and none of them had yet tried the Grameen approach to reducing it. The policy framework also seemed to be moving in the right direction. Both India and Vietnam were opening up their economies to the outside world and dismantling economic controls. Nepal was so keen on the Grameen model that it was planning two government development banks to implement it. Dr Getubig reported enthusiastically from Vietnam that the countryside was hopping with small enterprises, and that the potential reach of the 11 million member Women's Union was great.

> The government is encouraging the idea of microenterprise and credit for it.The whole environment is just right for replicating Grameen. The potential is enormous. The challenge is to provide the resources and the training so that they can do it successfully.[7]

APDC, Grameen Trust and CASHPOR worked together to provide the necessary resources and training. APDC gave US$25,000 to each project in two instalments, as returnable grants. Grameen Trust contributed around $35,000 to Nirdhan Nepal, SHARE and Nirdhan West Bengal and $21,000 to Tau Yew Mai. These were mainly on-lending funds at 2% and some operating funds, also as a returnable grant. The Vietnam project, Tau Yew Mai, which had other sources of funds, started operations in August, 1992 even before APDC funds arrived. The other three projects disbursed their first loans between March and July of 1993. In the event, however, GT funds were long delayed in all cases, so that projects actually juggled APDC funds to cover both operating costs and disbursement during their first year.

Staff training began in late 1992 with exposure visits for each project head and senior staff to AIM and the Grameen Bank. Tau Yew Mai leaders also trained with CARD and Project Dungganon in the Philippines, organized by Mr Aristotle Alip. In this way, the leaders of each project saw the model in its mature form in Bangladesh, but also experienced the rather different set of problems faced by the much younger replications in Southeast Asia. One of the major differences was the amount of staff skill and effort which must be put into motivating poor women to join, in a context where the project is new and unknown. Another was the importance of targeting in a society like Malaysia where the poor are a minority and harder to find than in a country of dense poverty like Bangladesh.

Throughout 1993-94, during the pilot period, the appropriate staff from each project attended the series of CASHPOR management development workshops on the basic Grameen skills of targeting poor women, creating credit discipline, financial management and planning, monitoring and evaluation. These were always hosted by a CASHPOR project member or by Grameen Bank, so that training took place in actual field conditions. The workshop series was initially funded by APDC-UNDP; in 1995, when APDC funding was running low, GT took over part of the cost and jointly organized the workshops with CASHPOR.

Except for Nirdhan, West Bengal, the projects were members of CASHPOR, which monitored their progress through quarterly reports, and offered technical assistance when this data indicated that problems were developing. Because of this relationship, APDC contracted the mid-term (end of the first year) and final (end of the second year) evaluations of each project to CASHPOR, so that these visits could be used for technical advice and assistance as well as simply reportage. The mid-term evaluations were done by experienced GB replicators, the founders of the earlier replications of AIM, ASHI in the Philippines and Savecred, Sri Lanka. Three of the final evaluations were done by Professor David S. Gibbons, the founder of AIM and its MD for its first seven years, and since 1993 Executive Trustee of CASHPOR. He was accompanied by Helen Todd, editor of the CASHPOR newsletter, *Credit for the Poor,* and author of a study of Grameen Bank borrowers, *Women at the Center.*[8] The final evaluation of Nirdhan West Bengal was done by two experienced senior staff from the Grameen Bank, who spent a month advising that project. In each case, the evaluators spent time in the field interviewing borrowers, observing centre meetings, checking financial procedures in the branch offices and discussing organization and policy with head office staff.

This book is partly a product of those evaluation visits. It brings together the mid-term and final evaluation reports, as presented to APDC, interviews with borrowers and staff, material written by the project leaders and case studies done by their staff. It is informed by the regular monitoring carried out by CASHPOR throughout the pilot phase of each project and up to the present.

The objective of putting all this material together into a book goes well beyond describing four GB-type credit programmes — although all are interesting in their own right and at least three have the potential to become full-scale Grameen Banks. By giving an unvarnished account of the problems encountered in the crucial first years of a credit programme it is hoped to alert all potential financial services practitioners to the pitfalls and obstacles they are likely to encounter. For this reason the technical detail contained in the reports, on such not-very-sexy subjects as cash control and interest rates, is retained. Second, this book provides the opportunity to analyse the *process* of creating these four programmes and to distill from this some lessons in best practice. These are discussed in the Conclusion.

Can It Work? Can It Grow?

SHARE, Nirdhan Nepal, Nirdhan West Bengal and Tau Yew Mai all agreed with APDC to implement the following objectives:

- to test the organizational and financial viability of the Grameen Bank financial system in the prevailing socio-economic conditions of each country, through a pilot project
- to determine the impact of the project on beneficiaries' income, employment and socioeconomic welfare
- and, to determine the feasibility of institutionalizing the pilot project into a full-scale credit programme for the poor to reach a large number of poor people in the country and help them overcome their poverty.[9]

Testing the model

Since CASHPOR was responsible for the evaluation of each project, its views shaped what was regarded as a proper 'test' of the viability of the Grameen Bank financial system. CASHPOR's Executive Trustee, Professor Gibbons, believes that the pilot projects should apply 100% Grameen Bank, and make changes only when they prove to be necessary. If the GB model is not faithfully applied, failure could be the result of the changes made, not the inapplicability of the model, he argues.

But he distinguishes between the 'essential Grameen', the 'coherent set of interrelated principles and procedures that delivers credit cost effectively to the poor,'[10] and non-essentials, like the saluting and exercises performed by GB borrowers, that can be adapted to the local culture. Innovations, which better fit the principles of the Grameen approach to the country context, should be encouraged.

The 'essential Grameen', very briefly described,[11] is an exclusive focus on the poor, with preference to poor women, simple loan procedures administered in the village, small loans repaid weekly and used for any income-generating activity chosen by the woman herself, collective responsibility through groups, bolstered by compulsory group savings, strict credit discipline and close supervision through weekly meetings and home visits. At project level the essential Grameen means a primary and single-minded focus on credit and savings. It includes rigorous, practical training of full-time staff, field-oriented management, political neutrality, open and transparent conduct of all business, setting an interest rate which will cover costs at full operation and aiming for financial viability.

A major part of the evaluation visits then, was to assess how 'faithfully' the Grameen Bank model was being applied and to point out deviations from it which should be corrected. SHARE and Nirdhan Nepal tried throughout their pilot project to apply 100% Grameen, although they were not always successful. Nirdhan Nepal flirted with a co-operative distributing fertilizer and other inputs, but got so burned that they returned to the narrow road of just financial services. In Vietnam, economic liberalization had created the market economy which is a precondition for operating a Grameen-type programme. But in a still monolithic political structure TYM initially opted to work through the existing commune framework, hiring Women's Union cadres as part-time field workers and relying on these officials to identify the poor. However, some painful experiences during the pilot project led the management towards GB methods of staff recruitment and training, and a re-emphasis on group and centre responsibility, in their third year. Only Nirdhan West Bengal decided from the outset to change the model to fit what it saw as special conditions in Bengal. They worked through brokers or 'facilitators' in the village and hired temporary untrained field staff. They sank funds into a joint venture with borrowers and planned the addition of health, training and literacy components to the credit delivery. As will be shown in the conclusion, Nirdhan West Bengal, while it certainly reached and benefited poor women, is the least successful of the four projects in terms of the final objective agreed with APDC — that of institutionalizing into a full-scale, viable programme to benefit large numbers of poor.

Grappling with problems on the ground, most projects came up with some interesting innovations. Nirdhan Nepal invented a livestock insurance fund to overcome the crises caused by the death of animals bought with their loans. SHARE staff, faced with the fears of desperately poor and illiterate women, made 'motivation folders', where the basic principles of SHARE were conveyed in symbols and pictures. And most of these replications adopted some of the innovations introduced by AIM for Malaysian conditions. The housing index, which AIM invented as a low-cost way to identify the poor through the kind of house they live in, was adapted to the house styles of northern Vietnam, the Nepalese *terai*, and the villages of India.

Contexts

Although all four projects dealt with different economic and political conditions, the main divide is between the projects in the Indian sub-continent and the one in Vietnam. Landlessness, and so dependence on daily labour for survival, is the basic economic condition of the poor in the Nepalese *terai*, in West Bengal and in Andhra Pradesh (although in the Nepalese mountains and in the rocky western districts of AP, some poor own some dry or infertile land). This landlessness forces women as well as men to take whatever daily labour they can get in the fields of the few landlords. In the Indianized culture which prevails in the Nepalese *terai* as well as in West Bengal and AP, this is a matter of shame for the women. Opportunities for daily labour are also seasonal and in most contexts there is a long, lean season when families go into debt to moneylenders in order to eat.

In Vietnam, nearly every rural family has usufruct right over a large houselot and some cropping land, although it may be infertile and they have little capital to boost its productivity. There are no cultural constraints on women working outside their homes, and nearly all women work the family fields and trade in the markets. Having access to land and playing active economic roles mean that Vietnamese women make rapid progress when they get access to credit. Before that happens, however, the consequences of their poverty are similar to those suffered by women in India and Nepal. Many poor Vietnamese women have to labour for others in order to survive and food-deficit households become deeply entangled in debt to moneylenders.

Most rural Vietnamese women are literate as well as more mobile than their Indian counterparts. In tradition and practice they have considerable control over the family budget. When they take loans from TYM they use them themselves and generally keep full control over the proceeds. This is not the case in either of the Indian projects, nor in Nirdhan Nepal. In all three projects, it is an uphill struggle to persuade the women borrowers to use their loans for their own income-earning activities and make their own decisions about reinvestment and the use of the profit. In the pilot phase this struggle had two fronts — one within the family of the borrower and the other within the mainly male staff of the projects. Most male staff in cultures which devalue women's economic contribution are slow to see the benefits which flow to the woman and her family from the borrower retaining control over her loans.

Targets and targeting

Targeting not only the poor, but the *poorest* amongst the poor, is fundamental to the Grameen model — and many of its strengths in credit discipline, group solidarity and impact on women rest on this base. Generally speaking, however, this bedrock of Grameen Banking was neither sufficiently emphasized in the project planning nor very rigorously applied on the ground. The projects set similar targets in actual numbers to be reached over the first two years. In the first year they each aimed to enrol 100 to 115 members, increasing in the second year to between 500 and 645.

However, the four differed quite markedly in how they would identify the poor and in their projected average loan size. Nirdhan Nepal had the 'loosest' criteria — families owning less than 0.5 of a hectare (rather than 0.5 of an *acre* as in Grameen Bank) qualified to join and it projected its average loan size during the two years to be US$100, considerably higher than equivalent borrowers in the Grameen Bank (at around US$50), or in any replication in Asia except for the projects in developed Malaysia. SHARE also defined the target poor fairly generously as those owning less than US$500 worth of assets and owning no more than one acre of dry land. When it began work in the arid western region of Andhra Pradesh it upped this ceiling to two acres of dry land. Its projected average loan size was more tightly targeted to the needs of very poor women, however, at US$50, half of that projected by Nirdhan Nepal.

Nirdhan West Bengal's project proposal was surprisingly vague on identifying the poor, saying merely that the beneficiaries should be 'at, near or below the poverty line' without defining it. But in practice, its actual average loan size of only US$36 in its first year, was one indicator (although not a stand-alone indicator) that it suceeded in hitting the poorest women. TYM's criteria, based on food sufficiency rather than income, were the most rigorous of the four. They considered only those families who earned the equivalent or less of 5 kg. of rice per capita, per month. Their asset cut off, however, was almost as high as SHARE's, at US$460. Its projected average loan was very low, at between US$20 and $30.

How these projects implemented these criteria in their selection of members and how much leakage developed to the non-poor is explored in the project chapters.

Impact

All projects were required to determine the impact of their project on their borrowers. Most argued it was 'too soon to show', and only TYM conducted a proper impact evaluation study at the end of the two-year pilot phase. Nirdhan Nepal commissioned an independent study which was completed in 1996 and was not available at the time of writing. The TYM study showed significant positive impact on both incomes and assets of the borrower's households. In Nirdhan West Bengal, the two-man Grameen Bank team conducted in-depth interviews with 25 borrowers and also found positive impact on incomes and the 'respect' the woman borrower enjoyed from other members of the household.

For SHARE and Nirdhan Nepal it is not possible to know accurately the impact of the programme on the borrowers, although field interviews were generally very positive. The exceptionally high repayment rates achieved by all four projects, is, of course, a strong indicator that the borrowers are benefiting, since only their desire to continue borrowing impels them to repay. The other proxy for impact is the demand from other poor women in the area to join the programme — in all contexts this demand was very strong just as soon as the demonstration effect of the first loans was felt. During the evaluation visits, evaluators looked for indications of gains in income and ownership of productive assets, and the level of living of the household as reflected in changes in food sufficiency, for instance, or reconstruction of houses and animal sheds. Impact studies were also expected to get some measure of the change in the woman's position in her household and her confidence in herself. They were concerned whether the loans led to a more productive use of the borrowers' time or simply added to already heavy work burdens. The partial information gathered on these issues is presented in the project chapters.

Signposts to Self-Sufficiency

That projects should work towards viability and independence of subsidies was fundamental to the thrust of APDC's Phase 111 Replication Programme. It was not expected, of course, that any of the pilot projects would reach viability within the two-year pilot period. The questions were: Were they on track to achieving it? How should it be measured?

The CASHPOR evaluations looked first at the efficiency measures which indicated whether project management was creating the capacity to reach self-sufficiency in a reasonable time and were forming new groups at a pace which would bring each branch to the point where the interest income earned by its operations would cover all of its operating costs. The most important of these measures is the cost per unit of money lent. The several authors in this book measure this in two ways. The first takes a ratio of operating cost over total disbursement for the period under review. The second, more demanding measure, takes operating costs as a ratio of average loans outstanding, that is the average amount actually out in the hands of the borrowers for that year. Since loans outstanding is a sharper measure of the continuing health of the programme, it is this second measure which is used in the concluding financial analysis. It was expected that cost ratios would decline, at least at branch level, with each succeeding year, as the number of borrowers serviced by the branch and the amount of lending — both total lending and average size of loan per borrower — increased. The objective of each branch was to bring the unit cost of each dollar disbursed down to below 20 cents.

A closely related measure of staff efficiency is the average number of borrowers served by each field staff. Fully utilized staff, in a computerized GB branch, bring financial services to a maximum of 400 borrowers each. This means that at full capacity the seven field assistants who staff a branch can serve 2,800 borrowers. The interest income from this fully covers the cost of the branch, including the cost of funds from head office. While a project is expanding these ratios will be much lower because its field staff include a large proportion of trainees — who do not form groups or disburse loans for the first six months of their training. Also, staff in a new project spend much more time motivating potential borrowers and training new groups than do staff in a mature Grameen Bank branch. As each branch reaches capacity, however, with seven trained field staff, its ratio should approach that of the Grameen Bank.

At project rather than branch level, these efficiency ratios slide backwards in the wrong direction whenever new staff are hired and trained in order to open new branches, because of the six-month time lag before they start forming groups and disbursing loans. However, when enough branches are formed and are operating at full capacity, head office will be able to recover its costs, including the cost of funds at market rates, which includes the cost of inflation.

The interrelated factors that project management has to get right in quickly moving towards financial self-sufficency are the rate and method of expansion, the financial services portfolio and setting the right interest rate on loans and deposits. All require different kinds of balancing acts. A too-rapid expansion in the number of borrowers can wreak havoc on the quality of credit discipline and targeting, since it is easier to recruit the non-poor than the risk-averse poorest. Since this can result in loan loss at unsustainable levels, it endangers the whole programme. Projects also have to decide whether to expand rapidly horizontally through opening large numbers of branches, or vertically by concentrating on building a few branches to viability. The first option reaches larger numbers of poor women more quickly, but keeps the project dependent for longer on large injections of subsidy from donors or governments — which may be arbitrarily withdrawn or invite political interference. CASHPOR has generally advised its members to expand vertically, although the outreach is slower, in order to establish credibility with banks and donors.

A varied loan portfolio, including general loans, housing loans, seasonal loans and tube-well loans, for example, increases income, but must be balanced against putting an unbearable burden of debt on borrowers before they are able to absorb more and larger loans.

An appropriate interest rate on loans to borrowers must cover all branch operating costs at full operation, including cost of funds at market rates, plus a modest net surplus to cover the head office and build reserves. The interest rate must be high enough to allow for loan loss (which for GB-type programmes should be no more than 3%), cost of funds including inflation, and operation cost, kept as low as possible by efficient use of staff. In South Asia and Vietnam during 1993 to 1995 inflation rates ranged between 6% and 10%. Taking this into account, a rate of at least 15% flat (or 30% effective) was found to be necessary to cover all costs. Most project heads, motivated by the ideal of 'helping the poor', were initially reluctant to charge rates as 'high' as were needed. Experience in the field, however, soon taught them that an effective rate of 30%, translated into weekly payments, was easily managed by their clients — and that their only competition, the moneylenders, were charging very much more.

Transforming NGOs

The leaders of most replications, and of the Grameen Bank itself, are convinced that governments cannot do Grameen Banking. Governments are too political — so they often cannot get the money back. Governments work through entrenched élites — so they seldom reach the poor. Government norms are too rigid and hierarchical to build the kind of village-centred, field-oriented organization required. But while most analysts will agree that governments are likely to fail, there is no such general agreement on the obverse — that NGOs will succeed.

Grameen Bank was a non-governmental organization which became a project of the Bangladesh Bank (not a very happy arrangement) and then grew into a specialized bank for the poor, governed by its own board, the majority of whom are representatives of its more than two million borrowers. AIM is a private trust, although governed by a board on which sit government appointees, and it has reached 40,000 borrowers, or nearly half of the hard-core poor in peninsular Malaysia. Both, in terms of outreach and impact, are undoubtedly successful. Grameen Bank has succeeded in attaining financial viability as well.[12]

However, none of the second generation of replicators in the Philippines and Indonesia have yet reached more than 10,000 members apiece, although they have been operating for almost eight years.

The main reason for this has been a chronic shortage of capacity-building funds. The bilateral donors who formed a consortium to finance the Grameen Bank's expansion, have not yet shown any major interest in the international replication/adaptation of its method of poverty reduction. To date, only relatively small amounts of funds have been made available. While this is no doubt due partly to lack of knowledge on the part of donors about the success and huge potential of the replication movement, the main obstacle is the huge amounts of funds that are required. The largest component of these funds is needed for on-lending. If on-lending funds could be sourced from commercial banks, the total needed the bridge the operating shortfall until projects achieved self-sufficiency would be much more manageable.

So the question for the third generation of GB replicators is what *kind* of NGO can transform itself into a specialized financial institution for poor women that can attract the participation of commercial banks? What kind of management can reach the numbers that would make the organization financially sustainable — and impact on regional or even national poverty rates?

The kind of management which succeeded in setting a course for expansion to institutional viability, and the kind that failed, will be discussed in detail in the project chapters and pulled together in the conclusion. What needs to be outlined here is what APDC, Grameen Trust and CASHPOR were *not* looking for when they worked together to identify four projects to fund in the third phase. They were not impressed with part-time, voluntarist leadership nor with NGOs whose focus was dispensing charity and welfare to women. They wanted organizations which were working in the field of poverty reduction and who accepted the importance and legitimacy of women's economic roles — and who were tough-minded enough to impose credit discipline on poor women. They did not want donor-dependent organizations, who thought only in terms of grants rather than paying their way with loans, and they preferred those who had the tenacity and national clout to raise some loan funds from domestic sources. Organizations with a political agenda, whether allied to political parties, or ruled by doctrinaire Marxism or fundamentalist religion were suspect.

But even given an NGO with none of these negative characteristics, the problem still remains: How can a well-meaning but essentially amateurish NGO transform itself into a specialized financial institution for the poor? The process traced with Nirdhan Nepal, SHARE in Andhra Pradesh, Nirdhan West

Bengal and Tau Yew Mai in Vietnam during their first two to three years of operation suggest some answers to this question. All followed a characteristic pattern, despite the different environments in which they operated. They all found a strong demand for credit amongst poor women, despite 'rumours' and élite resistance at village level (in all contexts except Vietnam). They all expanded rapidly in their first year as a result. This honeymoon period was characterized by staff euphoria and competition as to which field assistant and which branch could form the most groups. The second year, in contrast, was chastening as projects grappled with serious problems of centre discipline and staff delinquency. Out of these experiences the management of each project struggled to develop better methods of staff training and field supervision, the right mix of salary rewards and efficiency targets, professional systems of financial control — and finally, the kind of institutional form which could sustain the programme into a viable future. This is the story of the next four chapters.

Notes

1. Jayanta Kumar Ray, *To Chase a Miracle: A Study of the Grameen Bank in Bangladesh,* Dhaka, University Press Limited, 1987.
2. Other operating funds for Project Ikhtiar came from the Selangor State Government. On-lending funds were provided by an Islamic foundation, Yayasan Pembangunan Ekonomi Islam. An account of the pilot phase of 'Project Ikhtiar' is contained in Gibbons and Sukor, *Banking on the Rural Poor,* Penang, AIM, 1990.
3. Fuglesang and Chandler, *Participation as Process — What We Can Learn From Grameen Bank Bangladesh,* Dhaka, Grameen Bank, 1988.
4. Gibbons, 'Replication of Grameen Bank in People's Economies' paper presented to German Commission for Justice and Peace, Germany, November 1990.
5. Interview with Dr Mike Getubig, June 1996.
6. Tau Yew Mai Mid Term Evaluation Report, Feb-March 1994, p.1.
7. Quoted in FAXNET (now Credit for the Poor), June 1992. p.1.
8. Todd, *Women at the Center: Grameen Bank Borrowers After One Decade,* Westview Press, Boulder, Colorado, 1996.
9. Contract document between APDC and each project.
10. Gibbons (ed), *The Grameen Reader,* Grameen Trust, Dhaka, 1994, p.102.
11. For a full explanation of the 'essential Grameen' see *The Grameen Reader,* pp.101-103.
12. For studies on the impact of Grameen Bank see Todd, 1996, *Women at the Center.* On its sustainability, see Khandker, 1995, *Grameen Bank: Performance and Sustainability.*

1

Nirdhan Nepal

DAVID S. GIBBONS

NIRDHAN NEPAL DISBURSED its first loans in mid-March 1993, in the south-west plain that borders the Indian state of Uttar Pradesh. From the outset it had two advantages not possessed by the replications in India and Vietnam. Nirdhan's founder and Chairman, Dr Harihar Dev Pant, was the Deputy-Governor of the Nepal Rastra Bank, the central bank of Nepal. Its first Project Manager and most of its Board were commercial bankers. Nirdhan's leadership, therefore, were bankers by skills and training, but bankers whose experience had disillusioned them about the capacity of the formal banking system to reach and benefit the poor.

Nirdhan's second advantage was partly an outcome of the first. Nirdhan was registered as an NGO and consequently operated in relative freedom from government intervention. But, from its beginnings, it was licensed by the central bank to do 'limited banking', which gave a legal status to its lending and deposit-taking activities and made negotiating loans from commercial banks relatively straightforward. Its independence enabled it to implement the Grameen Bank methodology without the kind of compromises demanded by the party and government structure in Vietnam. It also ensured that its leadership remained in place through the drastic political changes in Nepal between 1994 and 1996. The two government-administered Grameen Bikas Banks, which operate at a much larger scale than Nirdhan in the western and eastern regions of Nepal, were severely affected by these upheavals. Both lost their chairmen and managing directors when the minority communist government came to power and both were again decapitated when it fell a year later. In the process, staff were politicized and split by the formation of party-aligned unions, and the recruitment of new members and the disbursement of loans levelled off.[1]

Poverty is far more widespread in Nepal than in India. Despite positive economic growth in the urban sector over the past decade, agriculture has remained stagnant and nine out of ten Nepalese live in the rural areas where infrastructure is lacking and illiteracy is the norm. Some 70% to 80% of the population is poor, and almost half the population, some nine million people, fall into the category of the hard-core poor. Poverty is most severe in the mountains of Nepal.[2] But Dr Pant decided that these scattered, inaccessible communities were too daunting a place to begin the Nirdhan project. So in January 1993, two managers and three female field assistants started work on the densely populated western *terai*, in the Rupandehi district.

The *terai* is a flat plain that runs like a band across the south of Nepal, bordering India. Unfortunately, flat does not mean fertile. The migration of hundreds of thousands of poor hill people into the *terai* over the past few decades has denuded the forest cover and led to degradation of the soil and frequent droughts. The productivity of land, which is anyhow very unequally distributed, has been dropping steadily.

Hema in Bairagenath village, a Magar from the hills 250 miles north of the project area, is fairly typical of recent migrant families settled on the *terai*. Her husband had no land and so they migrated here six years ago with her mother and their five children. They borrowed from a moneylender in the hills to buy three *kata* of land and repaid him gradually by selling firewood and doing daily labour and tailoring at night whenever they could get orders. But food and cash were always very short; their house is one of the most ramshackle in the village and 40-year-old Hema looks almost as worn and wrinkled as her mother.

Not surprisingly, there was a strong demand among such women, often pushed from behind by their husbands, to get access to Nirdhan loans, despite the usual rumours floated by the élites and moneylenders in the villages. Field assistant, Miss Lok Kumari Timilsina, working in the Siktohan Branch, recalls the first woman to show interest when Centre 3 was initiated in her village. Chandrabati Kebat had married into a large joint family of 27 members, who owned between them two *bigha* of land (3 acres). The couple tried to make a living by running a tiny retail shop.

> Of course, her husband was behind the decision and even helped her find other group members. Thus she became a member of group number 1...and was the first to receive her loan of Rs4,000 (US$82). (*Nirdhan News:* Jan. 1994.)

Nirdhan Nepal's work, during its two-year pilot project, was jointly funded by APDC, with a US$25,000 recoverable grant to cover operating costs, and by Grameen Trust, which committed US$35,000 as loan fund for on-lending to members. As part of its agreement with Nirdhan, APDC contracted CASHPOR Inc. to visit the project twice during the two-year pilot phase, to assess its progress in outreach and impact, report on how 'faithfully' it was replicating the Grameen Bank methodology, and to give advice and assistance to project staff. Key staff were trained in the series of Management Development Workshops organized by CASHPOR Inc. and funded first by APDC-UNDP and then by the

Key Replicator in Nepal

As Deputy Governor of the Nepal Rastra Bank, Nepal's central bank, Dr H.D. Pant was directly involved in three attempts to direct credit from commercial banks to low-income families. Although each had some initial impact on the access of poorer families to loans, in each case 'later it was found that most of the credit was not properly utilized, neither did it flow towards the low income group,' Dr Pant writes. This disillusionment with the ability of the formal banking sector to reach the poor led him on a search for a targeted alternative. In 1986 he visited Grameen Bank and was convinced that this was the relevant model. A decade later, Dr Pant's various efforts to introduce Grameen Banking in Nepal have resulted in a replication movement there which is more widespread in terms of both region and numbers than any country outside of Bangladesh.

'I tried to create some sort of Government sponsored formal banking institution to introduce the Grameen Bank Financial System concept in Nepal but failed to achieve [this] during the 1980s.' So in 1991, together with several other disillusioned development bankers, Dr Pant set up Nirdhan Nepal to replicate the Grameen Bank through an NGO. An assignment with the IMF took Dr Pant out of Nepal for two years, but in 1993 Nirdhan started its work in Rupandehi. In the meantime, the emergence of a governmental democratic system made it possible for his earlier proposal for a development bank to replicate Grameen to be dusted off and implemented. Led by Nepal Rastra Bank, two Grameen Banks were created in 1993, with Dr Pant initially Chairman of them both. In 1994, a retired DGM of the Agricultural Development Bank set up the Self-Help Banking Programme to replicate Grameen in eastern Nepal. So Nepal, by end-1994 had two government-sponsored Grameen Banks (and was planning to set up two more) and two NGOs replicating Grameen — together reaching over 14,000 families, and all expanding rapidly.

Beneath the urbane charm of the central banker, Dr Pant is an intense and determined man — which must be why he has overcome so many obstacles and done so much. When he enters a room, whether a staff meeting in Bhairahawa or a conference in Kathmandu, it is immediately clear how much respect he commands from people in Nepal.

When the Communist Party won the elections of 1994 and replaced the leadership of Nepal Rastra Bank (as well as in both government Grameen Banks), Dr Pant resigned in protest. He now spends a portion of his time in Rupandehi, living very simply above the project office in the dusty little town of Bhairahawa, directing Nirdhan's expansion. It is obvious which of his creations he believes is the right vehicle for replicating Grameen.

"In the case of government-sponsored banks, lack of flexibility and frequent political/administrative intervention could make GBFS ineffective...Given sufficient resources and good leadership, non-governmental banks or organisations appear to be more effective to achieve the desired objective of poverty alleviation.'

Source: **Paper presented by Dr Pant at 9th International Grameen Dialogue, Dhaka, 1994**

Grameen Trust. Management staff were also sent for exposure to Grameen Bank, to AIM, Malaysia, and to the two-month Area Managers' Training organized by Grameen Trust in 1995.

The First Year: Rapid Growth

The first evaluation was conducted by Dr Generoso Octavio, the founder of ASHI, the first Grameen Bank replication in the Philippines. He visited in December, 1993, when the project had been disbursing loans for almost nine months. He found that the project had already overachieved its membership and loan targets for the first year, with 155 women members in eight centres, and Rs420,000 (US$8,570) outstanding. Although it was too early to assess the impact of the loans, most of the women Octavio interviewed reported benefits from their first loan cycle. Octavio concluded that Nirdhan was 'on the right track' in reaching genuinely poor women and in faithfully replicating the Grameen Bank methodology.

He cautioned, however, about some weaknesses in group training and a too 'soft' approach to the group recognition test, which the newly trained group must pass in order to be admitted to the centre and become eligible for loans. He was critical of the lack of participation and discussion at the weekly centre meetings and the fact that the centre chief neither counted the collection before passing it over to the field assistant, nor signed the collection sheet.

> On targeting, Nirdhan is able to target the hard-core poor using the Means Test scheme of AIM. With substantially large numbers of potential members, the room for project expansion is very large, although a bit of caution is necessary so as to avoid the pitfall of losing the quality of the essential Grameen. In particular, if group formation is rushed up in order to meet targets, the quality of group members and the degree of motivation can be unduly affected.
>
> Although the [weekly centre] meeting was conducted in a business-like manner, the whole hour was not fully utilized. Recording of collections took quite some time leaving the mothers sitting on the floor doing nothing. It could have been well spent if the mothers discussed matters concerning attendance and tardiness, income-generating projects, problems faced by the groups and centre, plans and other related topics. (Assessment Visit Report 1994: 4-5.)

At field level, Dr Octavio advised project staff on tightening up cash control at centre level, by having the Centre Chief take responsibility for counting the cash and signing for it on the collection sheet and by issuing receipts to members as proof that their repayments reached the branch office.

Dr Octavio reported that Nirdhan Nepal, like nearly all replications in Asia, was experiencing some local opposition and harassment from moneylenders, although this was obviously not preventing the recruitment of new members. He also noticed that conditions were very tough for field staff. Even on the *terai* many villages were not accessible by four-wheel drive vehicles and there was no public transport. Field assistants travelled to their centres by bicycle, but distances were large and it sometimes took two hours in the rainy season to get to an early morning centre meeting.

At project level, he reported to CASHPOR that a major problem had arisen with funding. Since Grameen Trust funds had to be routed through UNCDF to the UNDP office in Nepal, the funds meant for on-lending only arrived eight months after loan disbursement began. As a result, Nirdhan spent its first year juggling the APDC funds for both on-lending and its rapidly growing staff costs. This cash crisis was partially resolved by the receipt of the first tranche of Grameen Trust funds in November 1993, and the second tranche of APDC funds in February 1994. It was resolved during 1994, with the negotiation of a Rs2 million line of credit from the Himalayan Bank, at 6% per annum. Over the next year, Nirdhan negotiated an additional Rs6 million in credits from four other commercial banks to finance its expansion. By 1996, 66% of Nirdhan's assets were funded from commercial sources — Nepalese banks and borrower savings.

Second Year: Problems Emerge

Two years after its first disbursement, Nirdhan Nepal had expanded to five branches and was reaching 1,240 members — nearly double its projection of 645 members under the pilot project. The pilot project target of Rs1,852 million to be disbursed in 644 small loans (average of Rs2875 or about US$59) had been greatly exceeded, with Rs6,355 million having been disbursed in 1350 small loans (averaging Rs4,707 or about US$96). Cumulative repayment was an excellent 100%. Savings were being mobilized, and individual, voluntary savings were also being encouraged. In March 1995, when Professor David Gibbons, Executive Trustee of CASHPOR Inc., visited Nirdhan Nepal to conduct the final evaluation visit for APDC, he concluded that in general the Nirdhan Nepal pilot project had been very successful. Clearly there was a strong demand among poor women for Nirdhan's loans and savings services, and Nirdhan had demonstrated its capacity to meet that demand, he reported.

Generally most of the members of Nirdhan Nepal appeared to be poor, judging from their housing conditions and limited holdings of agricultural land — especially in the Siktohan Branch. Some non-poor members were found in the field visit, but there does not seem to be much leakage to the non-poor. There is no priority, however, for reaching the poorest of the poor first. Nor are staff going from house to house to motivate the very poor to join the programme. Strictly speaking this violates the GB model, and, if not corrected, may lead to problems which could limit the impact of Nirdhan Nepal on poverty.

Several very poor households were visited who were not members, had never been visited by a Nirdhan staff member and didn't know much, if anything about the programme. A number of centres consisted of only 2 or 3 groups and expressed reluctance to admit the very poor in their villages in order to fill their centres.

Nirdhan's eligibility criteria seem high for rural conditions in Western Nepal. Households with less than 1 *bigha* (about 1.5 acres) of non-irrigated land or less than 0.75 acres of irrigated land are eligible to join. Although landlessness is rare in the area, these amounts appear to be a bit high. Probably, to give preference to the poorest of the poor, it would be better if the Project used one acre of non-irrigated land and half an acre of irrigated land, at least until all households in those categories had been given a chance to enter. Also of concern is Nirdhan's relatively high first loan ceiling at Rs5,000 (about US$100), which may tend to attract the non-poor and frighten the very poor. Its average loan size, at US$96, is also on the high side and indicates that it is not hitting the bottom of the poverty group.

Another problem with Nirdhan's targeting is its location in the *terai* near the Indian border; whereas the incidence of poverty is said to be much higher in the mountainous areas because of shortage of arable land and poor infrastructure. In fact many people have migrated from the mountains to the *terai* and opened land for cultivation. Looking at Nepal as a whole, there may be a danger that credit programmes for the poor, like Nirdhan, may aggravate the migration to the *terai* because they offer capital with which to develop the land. The relative absence of credit programmes for the poor in the mountains gives them less reason to stay there.

Women's Own Use of Loans

Although all of Nirdhan's borrowers are women, most of them do not use the loans themselves. A majority pass on their loans to their husbands. This is said, by the borrowers themselves and Nirdhan staff, to be Nepalese custom. The men are responsible for earning the household income and, in most cases, hold and manage the household finances. However, women borrowers, when asked how they could improve themselves and their position within the household if they passed on their loans to their husbands, agreed that it would be better to use at least part of the loans themselves. Moreover, they agreed that it was risky for the profits of the loans to be in the hands of their husbands given their greater tendency to spend on pleasure-seeking activities. Most of the women agreed that the household, especially the children, would tend to benefit more if they were in control of the profits.

However, the Nirdhan staff appeared to feel uneasy during these discussions and in subsequent debate among ourselves on the same issue. They felt that their work was hard enough already without taking on Nepalese tradition and culture. Anyway, some of them argued, this was a matter for husbands and wives to settle between themselves. Even the female staff were a bit slow to see the issue. Once they did, however, they too agreed it would be better for the women to use more of the loans themselves. The real feelings of the Nirdhan management, however, on this important issue were not clear.

The Grameen Bank requires that the loan be utilized by the borrower and that assets purchased with it become their property. As most borrowers are women, this tends to empower them. It insulates them also against abandonment and/or the taking of additional wives/mistresses by their husbands. We spoke to a woman borrower who had given her first and second loans plus a seasonal loan totalling altogether Rs18,000 to her husband to expand his grocery shop. It became more profitable and he used a large part of his increased income to bring a second, younger wife into the household.

When presented with this case, the male Branch Manager was astonished that we thought the woman had not benefited from her loans. He said the household income had increased substantially and she was enjoying a better level of living. When asked why the woman looked so distressed, however, he had to admit that her position in the household had changed disastrously.

Group Formation

Poor group formation is a problem at Nirdhan. In general, field staff appear to be too involved in it. Members are not forming their own groups and the conditions of group formation are not being followed carefully (for example, it is not uncommon to find close relatives in the same group). This may lead to serious problems in a repayment crisis. Borrowers may blame staff for putting unreliable members in their groups. Close relatives may collude with each other to deceive the project management.

Moreover, at least some group recognition tests (GRT) are not being taken seriously enough. They are being done by Branch Managers instead of a more senior officer. Nirdhan does not have an Area Manager as yet, so the Project Manager or his assistant should be doing the GRT. Moreover, checking for potential members' knowledge of and trust in each other is superficial. Questioning tends to concentrate on memory recall of rules, not on understanding and/or acceptance of them. Poorly formed groups and inadequately trained and tested borrowers will form a weak foundation for the programme.

Another important deviation from the GBFS is Nirdhan's failure to insist that centre chiefs and group officials are changed yearly. Staff say that the centres and groups do not want to change, so they have not forced them to do so. This is shortsighted and may result in centres and groups being captured and manipulated by their more capable members. Rules concerning the annual change of officials should be enforced.

Who Gets the Credit?

By Helen Todd

Sumita (not her real name), 35 years old, shifted downstairs recently to sleep with her mother-in-law. The loft where her husband sleeps is now occupied by a second wife. After 15 years of marriage and three children, Sumita is not happy with this development. 'We quarrel a lot. But what can I do? This is my fate,' she says.

Sumita has taken two quite large loans from Nirdhan Nepal — Rs5,000, and then Rs10,000. She gave both to her husband, who invested them in expanding his grocery shop. Sumita cannot tell us anything about the business. She cannot keep accounts and she directs all our questions to her husband. Her role in the family is to work the land that they own and to care for their buffalo and oxen. The increased profits from the grocery shop have enabled her husband to stock paddy, buy more livestock — and take a second wife. The benefit of membership for Sumita is not clear. She had already stopped doing daily labour before she joined Nirdhan; she admits they eat better; her children are doing well in school. But there is no doubt that much of the increased income from Sumita's loans will go towards establishing a second family, rather than to Sumita and her children.

In the same centre, a very poor woman, whose 11 and 12-year-old daughters are already out in the fields doing daily labour, has passed both of her loans to her husband for buffalo trading. She never sees the buffaloes and she never touches the money. Her neighbours, who are crowding into the tiny verandah while we talk, say the family eats more regularly. But the woman only says: 'I can't see any difference,' and begins to cry.

These two women live in Nepal. But there are women like them in every replication in Asia, including the Grameen Bank. They do not use even a portion of their loans themselves; they simply pipeline them to a male relative and they have no control over the proceeds. They are dependent on their husbands (or sons) for the repayment, just as they are dependent in all other aspects of their lives.

In the cultures of the Indian sub-continent this 'pipelining' seems almost expected — in striking contrast, say, to the women in the Tau Yu Mai project in Vietnam, who vigorously utilize all their loan capital. Amongst 40 women in the oldest centre of Nirdhan Nepal, 26 women passed all of their loan to their husbands or sons. Ten gave some to their husband but kept a portion for their own projects. Only four used all of the loan themselves — and two of these women were widows. Moreover, when I discuss this issue with the staff of the various replications, the common reaction is: 'What does it matter?' (Male staff). 'That is our culture' (Embarrassed laugh — female staff).

It matters. From the point of fairness — if we expect the woman to shoulder the burden of repayment then we should also be concerned that she benefits from the loans. But also, research by Gibbons and Todd on Grameen Bank borrowers,[3] and the work of other researchers, indicates that the impact of credit on poverty reduction will be slower if women do not retain control over loan use.

Moreover, all cultures are in a process of change; and Grameen-type projects, by targeting women, are catalysts for that change. In every project where I have interviewed borrowers there are women who are struggling — for good reasons — to change the 'custom' that denies them a voice in the family budget.

Take Fulmia, a member in the Sitalnagar Branch of Nirdhan Nepal. She is rushing to light her fire and feed her three children before they go to school. Because she is so busy with her children, her animals and the land they sharecrop, her husband, who drives a rickshaw, takes the milk from the buffalo she bought with her loan to the milk collection centre in town daily. The centre makes payment after 15 days. Does her husband also collect the milk money?

'No,' she replies emphatically, looking up from her cooking. 'I took this loan and I am responsible for repayment. So I need this money and I go and collect it myself. When I have repaid Nirdhan and bought feed for my buffalo, I save the balance. I have a dream to open a small shop on the roadside. My husband agrees with me, but this will be my own project. I will do it by combining my next loan with my milk savings.'

It is almost certain that Fulmia's family will rise out of poverty faster than Sumita's. In our research on 40 Grameen Bank borrowers in Tangail we found those families with the highest incomes and most assets were those where the wife played an active, and sometimes dominant, role in the household.

First and most obviously, two incomes are better than one. Sumita's loans have boosted the single source of earnings from her husband's grocery shop. But Fulmia has already added the sale of Rs40 worth of milk per day to the family earnings, independent of her husband's rickshaw earnings. When she is running a shop as well there will be three streams of income coming into this household.

Second, Fulmia exhibits the determination to save and reinvest which is so characteristic of poor women. When a poor woman who has experienced her children's hunger gets money in her own hands she is powerfully motivated to turn it into a tangible asset that directly contributes to the security of herself and her children — a store of paddy, a roof on the house, a cow or a new field to cultivate. Women who pipeline their loans and have no say in how the profits are used, must wait on their husband's decisions. It is now quite well established in the research literature that while most poor women will invest 100% of what they earn into the household, most men will keep back some proportion for their personal use and entertainment.

Opportunities for male spending of this kind are easy to spot in Nepalese villages. There is always a gambling circle on some verandah. Under the mango grove at the crossroads is a country liquor market open at night. Staff have tales to tell about husbands taking the loan money and disappearing into India — and other stories besides Sumita's of a rash of second wives. The 'vices' change from country to country, but the leakage of income by men is the same everywhere.

Impact on the Poor

As of February 1995 there had been no systematic impact evaluation study of Nirdhan Nepal. Nirdhan has prepared a series of case-studies, which show positive results, but there is no way of knowing with reasonable certainty how representative the case-studies are. However, interviews carried out during the field visit tended to confirm the widespread representativeness of the case-studies, particularly in the older Siktohan Branch and with borrowers who invested in milch buffaloes.

As most Nirdhan loans are being used by the husbands of the borrowers, they have become more fully employed and/or more gainfully employed as a result of the programme, resulting in higher incomes. Paradoxically this has released some of the women from the need to do daily labour on other peoples' land. Thus employment among some poor women may have been reduced and actually they may have beome more dependent upon their husbands.

Most borrowers said there had been some improvement in their level of living as a result of Nirdhan's loans, but not enough time had elapsed and not enough had been borrowed to result in a dramatic improvement. Probably the improvement in the socio-economic welfare of the households would have been greater if more of the women borrowers had utilized the loans themselves and kept control of the increased income. Drinking and gambling appear to be widespread vices in the villages.

Financial Viability

Nirdhan's operating costs at the time of the field visit were way beyond its income from interest earned from loans to the poor. For the six months from 15 July 1994 to 15 January 1995, Nirdhan's total operating costs were about Rs578,722 (around US$11,812), whereas its interest income actually received during that period was only Rs42,210 (about US$861). Thus interest income covered only about 7.3% of operating expenses. While it is not possible for Grameen Bank replication projects to break even during the pilot period, because the volume of lending is far too small, the fact that Nirdhan Nepal was still covering only 7% of its operating costs from its interest income in its third year of operation indicated that it was not on track for attaining financial viability in the near future. True, the percentage of operating expenditure covered by income had doubled from 3.5% for the year 16 July 1993 to 15 July 1994; but the proportion covered was still far too low.

As repayment (of principal and interest) had been perfect to date, none of the big difference between income and expenditure was due to loan losses. It was a function, therefore, of either excessively high costs, low scale of operation and/or an inappropriately low interest rate on loans to borrowers.

Step by Step to Higher Incomes

Chandramai and her husband stand at the side of a small sharecropped field and proudly point out their wheat crop, which stands a foot higher than the wheat around it. That is the impact of the seasonal loan she took two months ago to buy fertiliser. Nearby, on 6 *kata* of their own land, they have marked a place where they will sink a tube-well — using her tube-well loan — which will enable them to cultivate vegetables. With her general loan they bought a buffalo whose milk pays the instalments. It is a heavy burden, her husband says, and they still live in a bedraggled straw and mud house and worry about food. But step by step they are laying the basis for a higher income.

The majority of Nirdhan loans in the first and second cycles are going into livestock and cultivation and the increased income is used first on providing more adequate food and clothing for the women's families. In Centre 6 in Sitalnagar Branch, a member who bought a buffalo with her first loan is fairly typical of the newer Nirdhan members. She says: 'My husband gives me money for the household expenses, but it is never enough. Now I have bought a buffalo with my first loan I use the milk money to buy food and I can also pay the school fees and buy my five children some clothing.'

In the oldest and largest centre in Nirdhan's first branch, Siktohan, 40 women discuss the main impact access to loans has made on their lives. In the two years since the Centre was established its members have invested their loans in buffaloes for milk, oxen for ploughing, grocery shops, bicycle repair shops and cultivation. When they joined Nirdhan, most of them worked as daily labourers on the farms of big landlords — a matter of shame for women on the *terai*. But through their loan investments most of them have liberated themselves from daily wage labour and are now working for themselves and their families.

But poverty is entrenched in this region and these realists admit that building the assets and security which will lift their families out of poverty will not be quick or easy. Eight of these 40 women still must do daily labour to survive. One of them explains her situation:

I have been listening to everyone telling these visitors how much progress they have made, but progress is not so easy as they are saying. It is like you work so hard to cultivate a crop — you plough and put the fertilizer, but if there is no rainfall and your land is dry then you cannot get the harvest. I used my loan to buy oxen for ploughing, then after the season we sold them and bought a buffalo. But the milk is not enough, so now I am doing daily labour to cover my repayment. Our life does not change overnight.

Operating costs

Nirdhan's operating costs did *not* appear to be on the high side, with it costing them only a net of Rs0.21 to disburse one rupee to the poor as of mid-January, 1995. Staff expenses (including salaries and travel allowances) were the dominant expenditure (72% in the seven months to 15 January 1995 and the same percentage for the year from July 16 1993 to 15 July 1994). This is a relatively high proportion; most GBRs spend about two-thirds of outgoings on staff expenses. In the Project Proposal these were projected to average in total about Rs47,769 per month during the second year of operation, but actually they had averaged nearly Rs48,313 over the second year from 16 July, 1993 to 15 July 1994. However Nirdhan appeared to be keeping its other expenditures relatively low.

A closer look reveals that Nirdhan's operating expenditure was mainly incurred in laying the foundation for expansion of the programme. As of mid-January 1995, a total of 28 staff were employed by Nirdhan Nepal as compared to the nine that had been budgeted. Of the 10 non-budgeted staff, two were support staff in the Head Office and eight were trainees in the field. Both the Head Office and the branches had been strengthened for future expansion.

Despite this investment in future expansion, the net cost per rupee disbursed had averaged only Rs0.21 in the 7 months to 15 January 1995, compared to Rs0.46 in the second year of operation and to Rs0.57 during the first year — so efficiency had been increased substantially.

Interest rate

The nominal interest rate being charged to borrowers was 2% per month on a declining balance basis, collected in two equal instalments in the 51st and 52nd weeks of the loan period. However, as the principal has to be repaid at 2% per week, the average principal available to the borrower per month over the year-long loan period is only 54.2% of the amount borrowed. Actual interest paid is 13% of the amount borrowed. This results in an effective rate of interest to borrowers of 23.98%. However, taking into consideration that the interest is not payable until the end of the year and that the borrower can earn a return on it until it must be paid, an amount can be deducted from the interest actually paid. At 10% return on funds invested by borrowers, there would be a 1.3% deduction, yielding a net effective interest rate of of 22.68% to borrowers. However, to actually earn this on its loan fund, Nirdhan would have to keep it fully disbursed at all times — not an easy task with weekly repayment.

Nirdhan's effective rate of interest to its borrowers is relatively high for financial institutions in rural Nepal, as represented by the Agriculture Development Bank which was charging around 16% effective per annum. However, the latter was still heavily subsidized by government. While Nirdhan Nepal was subsidized by APDC and the Grameen Trust, it could not count on this continuing. Prudence, therefore, justified a relatively high effective interest rate to enable Nirdhan to break even sooner. In any case its borrowers still paid substantially less than the average interest of 37% per annum being charged by the informal sector lenders.

We reach the conclusion, therefore, that Nirdhan's low proportion of operating costs covered by interest income on loans to the poor is due primarily to its low scale of operation, but that it is laying the foundations in staff training to expand its outreach substantially.

Financial control

Financial administration and control are areas in which Nirdhan could improve considerably at both branch and centre levels. In a surprise check on the Siktohan Branch, we found a trainee simultaneously performing the roles of cashier, bookkeeper and custodian of the cash. Visits to other branches showed that in general there is no separation of these key functions in different hands at the branch-level in Nirdhan. The inadequate financial controls found by both Dr Octavio and Gibbons at centre and branch levels can be attributed to the high level of mutual trust and dedication felt by a small band of pioneer staff, so that dishonesty has become almost unthinkable amongst them. However, proper financial controls are essential as the project expands and current practice is bad training as well as an unacceptable temptation to new entrants.

At centre meetings also financial administration and control are too lax and disempowering to centre leaders. Centre chiefs do not, as a rule, count the cash collected before it is handed over to the field assistants, nor do they sign on the collection sheets or disbursement forms. There is, therefore, no village-level certification of original financial documents. No official receipts are sent to borrowers thus they cannot be sure their payments have reached the branch office. This leaves too much room for financial abuse. These are the same criticisms as were made by Dr Octavio, but as of March, 1995, they had not been remedied.

Expansion Potential of Nirdhan Nepal

Nirdhan is moving fast to cover the whole of the Rupandehi District. Already it has seven branches, including two that were opened on May 3 and August 23 1995 in Kapilvastu and Nawlaparasi districts, which are on the western and eastern side of Rupandehi district respectively. Once they are in full operation, say serving an average of 2000 poor households each, in 4 to 5 years time, then the Project will be reaching over 14,000 poor households in the District.

However, there is a danger in Nirdhan's method of expansion which may be called 'horizontal', establishing as many new branches as quickly as possible. The danger is that the heavy up-front operating costs of opening new branches and training additional fieldstaff may become too great for Nirdhan to bear in the 4 or 5 years it will take for these branches to break even. As of March 1995,

Nirdhan had secured funding until break-even only for its Shitalnagar Branch (from the Grameen Trust). While good performance at Shitalnagar should result in viability funding for other branches eventually, how is Nirdhan going to finance its rapidly increasing operating costs in the meantime? Probably it would have been more prudent for Nirdhan to put more emphasis on 'vertical' expansion, that is, on increasing the number of borrowers and total loans outstanding in say its first three branches until they reached financial viability, before opening new branches.

Institutionalization

A major advantage of Nirdhan Nepal, compared to most other GB replications throughout Asia, is that Nirdhan (like other NGOs in Nepal) is actually licensed by the Central Bank to do 'limited banking'. This legal status should make it easier for Nirdhan to become institutionalized and to raise funds, both domestically and internationally. It should also provide adequate protection to Nirdhan's borrowers — although exactly how the Central Bank intends to supervise the 'limited banking' is not yet clear.

Nirdhan fieldstaff have already dealt successfully with some crises, and this experience should make them able to deal with challenges in the future.

Nirdhan has also innovated successfully to handle problems peculiar to its location and dominant type of loans; as in its insurance scheme for the death of livestock. Some 35% of Nirdhan loans are taken for buying livestock — mainly milch buffaloes and oxen. These are large investments with good returns, but the risks are also large. If the animal dies the borrower can be left to repay a Rs5,000 loan with no income from her investment.

After several such experiences in their first year of operation, Project Manager, Mr Devendra Raut, decided to introduce an Animal Security Scheme. One per cent of the principal of all livestock loans is now deducted to make up an insurance fund. If the animal dies, the borrower gets 50% of the value of the loan to begin another project. So far, this animal insurance scheme has paid out Rs4,450 for eight dead animals — three pigs, four goats and one buffalo. The fund needs to grow larger before it can cover all risks without loss to the project. In March, 1995, it had a balance of Rs4,012. But the concept offers a needed safety net and is very popular amongst Nirdhan members.

Preparing the Way For Scaling Up

CASHPOR reported to APDC that Nirdhan Nepal's pilot project was a success. It had shown that the Grameen Bank model could work in the context of Nepal (at least in the *terai*). It had outperformed its targets in outreach and disbursement and its repayment rate was still 100% after two years. As far as could be gauged from field interviews, it was helping poor women raise the incomes of their households. Nevertheless, the project had some serious

Teamwork and Problem Solving

When Govind Pandey was appointed Branch Manager of Dhakdhai Branch last November, the branch was in bad shape. The previous manager (no longer with Project Nirdhan) had neglected the field work, and discipline in the centres was collapsing.

'Members would wander in half an hour late or not come at all, sending their instalments with their husband or another member,' Govind remembers.

The previous field assistants were transferred and Govind started with a new team — two women trainees and two men. They all live in the bare, one-story branch office building, do their own washing and cooking, and cycle up to 10 miles to attend 7.00 a.m. centre meetings. Four months later there is a great atmosphere of comradeship and commitment in this branch.

Govind and his keen young team have formed 31 new groups in those four months and discipline has been restored in all centres. Govind explains his strategy for getting the branch back on track.

When everyone is bad it is important to balance penalties with new facilities. You cannot just dish out punishments and expect members to come back to the meetings. First, I insisted on compulsory attendance at weekly meetings. We refused to accept instalments until everyone was present. Sometimes we waited three hours. So then the early ones quarrelled with the latecomers and that put pressure on all to attend. If the meeting time was not convenient we allowed them to change it, but they must be there. In really bad centres we refused to discuss loan proposals until attendance improved.

Second, I had to ensure perfect discipline amongst the staff, which was lacking before. They must be punctual. So I visited four or five centres a day to properly supervise their work.

Then as soon as attendance improved, I introduced new kinds of loans. There were no group fund loans allowed before, so we started those. And we introduced seasonal loans and tube-well loans. But we gave them only to members with good attendance. Then we could point to those members and say: 'See. If you follow the rules like them you will also get these new loans.'

While Govind is talking, one of his trainees comes cycling in the gate. After she has washed the sweat from her face and the dust from her feet at the pump, she talks about her morning. She left at 6.00 a.m. to reach her centre meeting on time. But the 10 members were all there and all punctual. Then she went to a neighbouring village to begin training a new group. But she discovered that four of these five women had outstanding loans from an agricultural bank, so she had to tell them they were disqualified. 'Clear your loans, then we can consider you again,' she told them.

'So tomorrow I'll just have to start again from scratch finding another group,' she laughed, throwing up her hands. 'But I'm a Gurkha. My father was a soldier. We don't give up so easily!'

weaknesses that needed to be corrected before the final objective of institutionalizing into a full-scale credit programme could be realized. Once the quality of group formation had been improved and financial administration and control tightened, Nirdhan would be ready to scale-up to reach large numbers of poor women and their families throughout western Nepal.

Professor Gibbons advised that Nirdhan's impact on the very poor would be improved further by giving preference to the very poorest women and their families. Its impact on family welfare and the status of women would be enhanced by insisting that women borrowers use the loans themselves and that they own the assets bought with the loans in their own names.

He urged Nirdhan to create as soon as possible a master plan for expansion and the attainment of viability, including a suitable strategy for expansion into the hills and mountains. Such a plan would set targets for staff so that they are motivated to reach their full capacity. Probably their salaries and means of transport would need to be reviewed and improved, so that staff can see their work with Nirdhan as a long-term career.

In the wake of the final evaluation report, Nirdhan instituted a number of changes in financial procedures and group formation:

Cash control — Financial control was tightened at branch level by separating the functions of branch manager and accountant. Both hold keys to the cash box. The manager is responsible for the cash; but when depositing and withdrawing, both manager and cashier have to sign the papers. At the centre meeting the collection, savings and disbursements amounts are announced at the end of the meeting and the centre chief retains one copy of the receipt signed by the field assistant. A second copy is signed at the branch office to prove that the collection was received by the branch and is returned to the centre the next week. The new system minimizes the possibility of staff dishonesty and gives more authority to the centre leaders.

Reaching the poorest — Each branch office is asked to prepare a list of the poor people in every village which the field staff use to motivate women to join Nirdhan. The staff check whether per capita income per month is over Rs280 (US$6), a much more rigorous means testing than Nirdhan applied before. The land ceiling for membership was reduced from 1.5 acres of non-irrigated land to one acre and from 0.75 acres of irrigated land to 0.5 acres. Field staff were told to encourage poor women to form their own groups and not to intervene unless the proposed member was not qualified.

Dr Pant reported with great satisfaction:

> When we introduced this system the field staff argued that there were no more poor people other than the ones already in the centres. But when they started to go house-to-house through the villages they found the poor were there.[4]

Loan use — Nirdhan made it a rule that the borrowers utilize the loan themselves and assets purchased with it become their property. Staff were motivated to implement this rule.

Expansion plans — Nirdhan decided to expand the project vertically — that is, to fill up the existing branches first and to open a minimal number of new branches. In 1995 Nirdhan recruited another 17 field staff and four managerial/accounts staff to make a staff total of 52. Early in 1996 it opened an area office to strengthen the supervision of branch staff.

By March 1996, Nirdhan Nepal had 2,529 members and was growing at around 18% per quarter, a better outreach than any of the other replications featured in this book. Its branches were making good progress towards viability. The oldest branch, Siktohan, was able to cover all of its operational costs by the end of 1995 and two more branches, including one funded by Grameen Trust as a package to viability, are expected to become operationally viable by April 1997. Defaults were still zero.

The decision to open seven branches, a fairly moderate kind of horizontal expansion, turned out to be a good one, because of Dr Pant's financial acumen and connections. Only one branch was fully funded; one was already covering its costs. Dr Pant was able to secure all the on-lending funds he needed from commercial banks, under the priority lending regulations he himself had put in place during his time at the Central Bank. He negotiated Rs10 million from various commercial banks at 6%. He put enough of this into bonds and fixed deposit at 10% to 12% to cover the shortfall in operating expenses for his remaining five branches from the interest spread. Nirdhan Nepal is currently funding more than two-thirds of its costs from commercial sources and its members' savings — the only young replication in Asia to achieve this.

But despite all the good news in the statistics, Nirdhan was still having some difficulties maintaining staff and centre discipline on the ground. When the Grameen Bank Zonal Manager for Comilla spent time in the branches in May, 1996, on behalf of Grameen Trust, he found that group formation was still weak in some branches, with no checks on the member's poverty status before admitting them to the centres.

This indicated that Nirdhan's major weakness — the looseness of its targeting and leakage to the not-so-poor — was not being rectified in the field. The lowering of the income criteria for admitting members, in order to reach the very poorest, which was instituted by Dr Pant in 1995, was an empty formality without a parallel tightening in the field supervision, through a rigorous group recognition test and visits to the houses of potential members.

The Grameen Bank Zonal Manager also found a number of members in one branch who were irregular in their payments and not attending meetings, but these danger signs were not being reported by the branch to head office, so no remedial action could be taken. He strongly advised that monitoring be improved, so that full information on overdues and centre attendance be reported. He also advised that achievement targets should be set for all staff so that they are fully utilized.

Some branch managers were fighting back against this breakdown in discipline, Dr Pant reported. When the new branch manager of Siktohan, the oldest branch, found many members not attending meetings, he stopped disbursement until attendance improved. Dr Pant decided to take the most problematic branch and merge it with its successful neighbour, while hiving off part of that branch into Siktohan, which was already viable and running well.

Staff efficiency in Nirdhan was fairly low, although this is partly explained by the number of still non-productive trainees. Its 29 field staff were handling only an average of 106 members each. At full capacity, they should be servicing at least 300 borrowers, whose interest income would fully cover the costs of delivering them credit. Despite this low utilization of staff, Nirdhan's costs per unit of loan disbursed were the lowest of all the four replications, at only 20 cents per dollar disbursed. One of the reasons for low costs was that staff salaries were relatively low. Although nowhere near as low as staff cost at TYM in Vietnam, staff salaries at Nirdhan, by end 1995, made up only 54% of total expenditure, compared to around 75% for SHARE. There is no doubt a relationship between low staff salaries and low staff output, which could be reversed by improving the salary package for Nirdhan staff.

1996 saw some developments on the national scene, which improved the context in which Nirdhan functioned. The new government passed the Development Bank Act, which enables NGOs doing limited banking like Nirdhan to register as a full-fledged development bank. Nirdhan plans to reform itself as a bank, called Nirdhan Bikas Bank. This institutionalization as a bank should make it easier to acquire funds for further expansion.

At the same time Nirdhan hosted a meeting of all the Grameen Bank replications in Nepal, including the four government-owned Grameen Bikas banks and an NGO, Centre for Self-Help Development, which resulted in the formation of the National Network of GBRs in Nepal, Grameen Network Nepal (GNN). This network should improve co-ordination between all the on-going governmental and non-governmental efforts to deliver credit to the poor in Nepal, and iron out some of the rivalries which exist between their field workers on the ground. It will also enable replicators to lobby for financing from both governments and international agencies.

Notes

1. Interviews with Mr Ramesh Poudyal, Managing Director of Grameen Bikas Bank, Biratnagar, and his Deputy, Mr Deepak Sharma, during a field visit in May 1996. Mr Ramesh was summarily removed from his post the same month, for the second time.
2. Dr D.H. Pant, paper presented to the 9th International Grameen Dialogue, Dhaka, 1994. David Seddon, *Nepal, A State of Poverty,* Vikas Publishing House, New Delhi, 1993.
3. Todd, *Women at the Center* pp. 46–8, 65–6.
4. Interview with Dr Pant, Kathmandu, May 1996.

Figure 1.1: Growth of Members and Loans

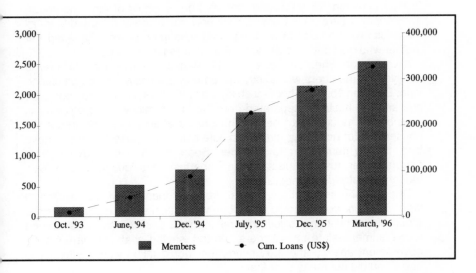

Figure 1.2: Growth of Branches and Staff

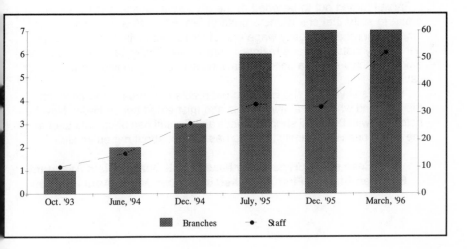

Barsati wins Love and Livelihood from her Grocery Shop

Barsati Mallahin, 25 years old, comes from a family of nine members, traditionally fishermen in Sunwal. With only one *bigha* of denuded land, all the adults were forced to work as hired labourers, which weakened her mother who died in childbirth when Barsati was ten years old.

A year later, when she was only 11, Basati was married into a large family of 15 members who jointly owned only a small piece of homestead land. She was 15 when her first child, a daughter, was born and soon after she and her husband separated from the joint family with no property of their own. She could not get her husband's affection and he frequently abused her for not giving him a son. Life became impossible as she gave birth to one daughter after another. Soon after the birth of her third daughter, her husband beat her until she lost consciousness. She even thought of suicide in desperation.

One day she heard about Nirdhan from her friends and was excited to learn that poor people could get a loan without collateral. But she was too afraid of her husband to join the training sessions and she was worried when some well-to-do villagers started saying that Nirdhan was a government agency and the government would take away anything you had if you did not repay their loans.

But after a few of her neighbours joined Nirdhan and started going to the group training, Barsati got up enough courage to join Group 2 of the Dhol Bajuwa Center. After they passed their group recognition test she was the first in her group to be recommended for a loan and the center meeting approved credit of Rs2,000 for her to start a retail shop.

Barsati turned out to be good at the grocery business and today she is proud to state that she earns a profit of around Rs40 a day, which is 2.5 times higher than the daily wage rate of Rs16. With this income, she pays her weekly instalment and maintains her family. She is also saving a small amount each week in a personal savings account, in addition to her group savings.

She says shyly that she has also been able to win back the affection of the husband who only a few months ago mistreated her so badly. Now he helps her with the retail shop business and Barsati has been able to obtain the family peace and amity that she has dreamt about her entire life.

Case study prepared by Miss Shanti Dhakal, Field Assistant, Siktohan Branch. First published in *Nirdhan News*, April-July 1994

2

SHARE, Andhra Pradesh

DAVID S. GIBBONS

SHARE, THE FIRST ATTEMPT at a thorough-going replication of the Grameen Bank model in India, disbursed its first loans in the Kurnool District of Andhra Pradesh in May 1993. Its subsequent success — and the personality and drive of its founder — have made it a central player in the growing replication movement on the sub-continent.

SHARE's founder and Managing Director, Mr M. Udaia Kumar, comes from a background of financial management and NGO work. What he decided to implement in Andhra Pradesh was by-the-book Grameen Banking, making adjustments to the local conditions only when experience showed these to be imperative. In the event, few adaptations had to be made.

The SHARE replication was meticulously planned and organized, well before it started work on the ground. Four of its senior staff spent a month training at AIM in Malaysia at the end of 1992, funded by APDC. Early in 1993, three of them did a further training stint with Grameen Bank, supported by Grameen Trust. This team surveyed six districts, selecting the two neediest in very different regions of Andhra Pradesh to test the robustness of the model. A visit to the field during the time of site selection and staff recruitment by Professor David Gibbons, MD of AIM, helped to refine and clarify the methodology and shape the pilot project proposal. This proposal got the support of APDC and Grameen Trust who promised both operating funds and revolving loan funds over a two-year period.

SHARE's vision was ambitious, but its initial implementation was fairly cautious.

Our objective is to reach all the districts in the State of Andhra Pradesh, within a span of few years. At the same time we do not wish to run matters in a hurry but to start a few branches and after they are strong footed, we would take a swift strong sweep to reach as many villages as possible. (SHARE Annual Report, Nov. 1992-Aug. 1993.)

However, the preparation and planning that preceded the field work meant that once the two branches got underway in mid-1993, with additional field staff, they made rapid progress. They were able to reach their two-year targets in both members and disbursement within the first year of operations and during that period they did not experience a single default.

The implementation of SHARE and its notable early success illustrate a lesson which has been learned in all the efforts to replicate the Grameen Bank model in various countries of Asia. Capable and determined leadership at the beginning of the project is crucial and this leadership must be able to work full-time in the field. In Mr Udaia Kumar, SHARE certainly had this kind of leadership. In 1993, he resigned from his earlier commitment as Executive Secretary of Progress, a scientific NGO, and devoted his full energies to the SHARE credit programme.

First Hurdles

Despite his careful planning, the first problem Mr Udaia faced was the non-arrival of promised funding. Despite being registered by the Ministry of Home Affairs to receive foreign funding, permission from the Ministry of Finance to receive the Grameen Trust loan for on-lending was delayed for 18 months. (Grants do not require this permission.) The first tranche of funds from APDC was sent by telegraphic transfer in March 1993, and lost in the bowels of the banking system for 15 months! SHARE funded its first few months of operation and disbursement with loans raised from friends, while appealing to APDC, which was flexible enough to send the second tranche of funds almost a year ahead of schedule.

Even while this high-wire act was going on, SHARE staff were beginning to hit up against élite resistance in the villages.

> Villages are governed and controlled by village heads who are not only political leaders but play a pivotal role in every sphere of a villager's life. The *sarpanch* of a certain village informed about our activities to some anti-social elements [armed thugs] who threatened our staff in various ways.
>
> Since the SHARE programme is to focus on women, there were whispering campaigns about our intentions. (Annual Report, Nov.1992-Aug. 1993.)
>
> Work could not progress freely and without hindrance as the villagers depended on the leaders for their daily needs. In some villages the permission of the leaders had to be first taken, and when it was sought for, it was bluntly refused. It therefore became quite impossible for the staff to even enter certain villages. (Annual Report, April 1993-March 1994.)

SHARE staff found that some women who were too landed to qualify for membership became so annoyed that they discouraged poorer women from joining. But as SHARE continued its work some of this resistance faded and a strong demand began to emerge amongst poor women.

Origins

When Mr Udaia Kumar flew to Dhaka in November 1991 to attend the 2nd International Dialogue at Grameen Bank, he was, as usual, well prepared. In his pocket was a proposal to set up a rural credit project in Andhra Pradesh. In Dhaka he found Professor Yunus and the Grameen Trust very interested to support the first Grameen replication in India. There was only one problem. The night before he left Hyderabad, the Board of Progress, the NGO of which he was Executive Secretary, told him that they did not want this project — credit was too risky and could sully the good name of their scientific NGO, they said. So Udaia had a project and a promise of funding — but no organization. That was when he took SHARE (registered to start a school which hadn't happened yet), dusted it off and made it the vehicle of a Grameen replication, which, three years later, is training other NGOs in India interested in Grameen Banking.

Udaia, trained as an accountant, has extensive experience in the training and technical assistance side of NGO work. As head of Progress he organized mammoth training workshops and conferences for NGOs and grassroots groups in activities designed to head-start technological change in depressed areas. He is good at this. He bustles and gets things done; he is genial and tireless; people like to work with him and he has contacts all over India. So, as he describes it, plenty of rupees got spent; his Board was happy; the donors were happy. Only Udaia was not happy. In all this work, he was increasingly looking for impact on the ground — and was increasingly frustrated at not finding it.

He organized training for many women in growing blue-green algae, for example. It was a big success. But when the women went home none of them did it. A major reason was their lack of capital. It was at this point, at a conference in Bangkok, that Udaia heard about the Grameen Bank. It sounded like the kind of direct intervention, with concrete results on the lives of poor families, that he was looking for.

Udaia is now full-time MD of SHARE (he resigned from Progress in 1993) and runs his two branches, each 200km from Hyderabad in opposite directions, from an office annexe to his house. The big white 4WD is gone; he travels by bus and train to the branches and then gets around on the mopeds of his field staff.

But in the often violent world of rural Andhra Pradesh, nobody gives him any hassles. With his burly form and bushy moustache, he looks more like a policeman than an accountant. With his staff, he is more likely to have his arm around a field worker's shoulder, sharing a joke, than to be giving a lecture.

SHARE is hosting increasing numbers of visitors and trainees — other NGOs in India who want to use the GB method to deliver earning power to poor women and who are learning from SHARE how to do it.

After we had established two branches and SHARE staff visited these villages continuously, people started understanding that we are committed to what we speak. Now we find a lot of demand from the neighbouring villages, and there are many who come and knock at the SHARE office to come and open centres at their places. (Annual Report, Nov. 1992-Aug. 1993.)

Region of Water; Region of Stones

There are three distinct climatic zones in Andhra Pradesh, and SHARE is operating in the two extremes, which shapes how its women members use their loans. Dachepally Branch in Guntur district is on the inland edge of the fertile coastal plains irrigated from the Krishna River. Two crops of paddy are possible here as well as many vegetable crops and cotton. There is plenty of fodder for animals and government milk collection centres service every village. Unlike many rural areas, daily labourers in this area, men and women, can get work throughout the year.

Although most land is owned by a handful of rich landlords, landless families can get access to land to cultivate, provided they have capital for inputs and, preferably, oxen for ploughing. Landlords will not rent their land, since they fear losing it under various 'land to tenants' laws. Instead there is a leasehold system which works like rent, with the lease price paid at the time of harvest in a fixed number of bags of paddy. Although cultivators can get a second crop in many fields, the cost of irrigation, through the hire of pumps and water charges, is high, so irrigation is possible only for families with access to capital.

The first and second cycle loans in the Dachepally Branch reflect the considerable opportunities of this ecosystem. More than two-thirds of all loans have gone into livestock — and 77% of the livestock loans are in milch buffaloes. Goats, sheep, pigs and ram lambs make up most of the remainder. Off-farm trading takes up most of the remaining third of the loans, concentrated in sundry shops and tailoring. Some 36 of the 460 loans have been taken for hawking of agricultural produce like chillies, vegetables and fruit. Although no loans have so far gone into leasehold land, interviews with a number of borrowers revealed that the additional income the women are getting through milk has enabled some of their husbands to expand the amount of land they are able to lease. Several borrowers said that they planned to put future loans into financing the acquisition of leasehold paddy land.

Dachepally is the second branch established by SHARE. But Mr Udaia Kumar selected it as the branch to scale-up to viability because of this climate of economic opportunity. Expansion is rapid here — the number of members grew from 60 to 435 in 1994 — and most members are eagerly taking the maximum loan size of Rs2,000 (US$65) for the first loan and Rs3,500 (US$113) for the second.

Veldurti, SHARE's first branch, is in an entirely different climatic area in the south-west of Andhra Pradesh. This is a drought-prone zone; its soils are rocky

Thieves, Thugs and Other NGOs

In Narasapuram, a village near Veldurti, the *sarpanch* had been away for a long time. The staff motivated and formed a group in his absence and without his permission.Then the *sarpanch* returned and the group broke up within five days because of his resistance. The reason for his negative attitude was because of an incident which took place earlier. Another NGO called Young India Project (YIP) had taken photographs and collected Rs30 to Rs60 from the villagers saying that they would distribute lands. Those who had paid the money were taken to the Mandal Revenue Office and made to stage a *dharna*. One of the objectives of YIP is to form groups and make them fight against the exploitation of the poor by arranging rallies and make the villagers claim their rights. Therefore, the *sarpanch* forbade anyone in the village to give money to, or to take loans from, any outsiders.

We talked to the leader and slowly, because our pledge promises that we even refuse a glass of water from the villagers, our sincerity was accepted and we could finally establish groups in this village.

Kurnool District has many factional villages. In some places the fear of the villagers is so great that they hesitate to take up any loan project. Allugundu, where we have a centre, has a bitter feud with a neighbouring village. This originated in an election rivalry between the two village leaders and has resulted in several murders. In November 1993, a mob attacked with knives and axes and looted and burned many houses. Four SHARE members lost all their belongings, including sewing machines and a grocery shop financed by their loans. SHARE staff went immediately to the village. Loan repayments were frozen for three months for affected members and two were given emergency loans to restart destroyed projects. Others were helped to rebuild their houses.

Other centres were mobilized to help, even in the far away centres in Dachepally, and willingly contributed money and clothing to the centre in Allugundu — an important social awakening on all sides.

Source: **SHARE Annual Report, 1992-3**

and infertile. Like Rangpur in Bangladesh, only one crop a year is possible and in the long, dry summer months before the monsoon there is little work and less fodder. This is when the men migrate to other districts and their families and animals left behind go hungry.

As in Dachepally, most SHARE loans in Veldurti Branch are going into livestock, but not many for milch buffaloes; most of the members are fattening ram lambs. It is more difficult in this district to find enough fodder for buffaloes through the dry season and there is no milk collection centre close to the village.

But if ram lambs are less demanding, they are also give no income until they are sold at six months. So most Veldurti members must find their weekly repayment out of their already painfully stretched daily earnings.

As a result, most members take small loans the first time (average Rs1,287 or US$41) and their second loans are not much bigger. It costs around Rs1,000 for two ram lambs. If they buy more than two, not only do they face a bigger weekly repayment but they have to find more fodder.

Branch staff report that the few wealthy landlords in this area keep a grip on the poor through their control over opportunities for daily labour. In several villages where staff did motivation work, villagers refused to consider joining SHARE without permission from the local landlord, so SHARE was forced to postpone centre formation in those villages. At the existing centres, several women explained that they cannot build up their lamb flocks because of hostility from the landlords on whom they depend for daily labour.

'If I take more than two lambs with me to work, the landlord complains about the "big crowd", and I can't leave them at home because there is no fodder,' a member explained.

Mr Udaia Kumar reports that motivation work in Veldurti was initially very tough for the SHARE staff.

> The morale of the people is very low, so that even when opportunities come their way people hesitate to take up any offer. They lack the confidence to take the seed money as they don't trust their repayment capacity. The SHARE staff put in much hard work persisting in their patient goading. (Annual Report, April 1993-March 1994.)

However, many families in Veldurti, unlike Dachepally, have some land — but dry land on which they grow only maize or groundnuts dependent on rainfall. The women say they could use capital for seedlings and ploughing to cultivate crops. But returns on cropping are also seasonal — so the same problem they face with fattening livestock confronts them with cultivation — they cannot take the capital they need from SHARE because the weekly repayment must be met from straightened daily income.

This bony land and its pitiless climate means that the impact of credit will take longer to show in the lives of these very poor families. What seems to be happening in the first one or two loan cycles is that most women are simply stabilizing their food supply. Many take loans from SHARE and buy two ram lambs which they fatten for six months and then sell at the beginning of the dry season. The proceeds are used to keep the family going during the five months when there is no work in the village.

It might take several loans before the poorest women have the basic food security which would enable them to invest in assets which would lead to higher earnings, which could then be used to build up more assets, and so on, in the classic Grameen Bank process which eventually liberates families from poverty. But there are hopeful signs that this process is beginning.

Investing in Courage

Poverty is deep and entrenched in Veldurti villages. In the Narlapuram centre meeting, the women's *saris* are so worn and faded it is hard to see what was the original colour. Their hair has the dry and rusty look of chronic malnutrition. They work daily in the fields of one or two landlords, but for five months between February and June there is no work and their husbands leave the village to do construction work in the district capital at Kurnool.

Most women in the Veldurti centres take very small first loans and use the proceeds for the most basic needs. For example, when Thippamma sold her ram lambs in the last dry season, she was too poor to roll her capital. She used the proceeds to buy clothes for her children and a wooden door for her house. The balance helped them with food through the dry season.

But gradually some of the centre members are getting up the courage to take bigger loans and reinvest them. Pullamma was so afraid of repayment she took only Rs500 (US$16) for her first two loans, and bought goats. To make it worse, her house was burned down in the raid a year ago. But now her house has been rebuilt, with some help from the government. She and her husband, and recently her eldest son, are all doing daily labour. So for her next loan, she plans to take Rs2,000 and buy a buffalo, confident that she can keep up the repayment and buy fodder over the dry season, with their combined incomes from milk and wages.

The leader of her group was more daring from the beginning. She bought a cow for Rs1,000. Then she opened a tiny tea shop which uses all the milk her cow can produce. She makes an average of Rs50 per day from her shop, compared to the Rs25 per day she used to make hawking vegetables. She aims to take a second loan of Rs2,500 to expand the teashop into a restaurant. 'I will have no problem repaying that amount,' she said.

The secretary of the Allugunda centre also shows a gradual building of assets and income which will probably headstart her family out of poverty over the next few years. With her first loan of Rs1,000 she bought a poor quality buffalo. After a year she sold it and put the money together with her second loan, also of Rs1,000, to buy a better buffalo, which is now giving her two litres of milk daily. This family has two acres of dry land and five children at home. Her plan for her third loan is to capitalize these two assets, the land and their labour supply, to produce a more consistent income. She aims to buy an electric pump for Rs5,000 which will enable the family to irrigate the land and cultivate vegetables all year round.

Veldurti Branch is something of a test for SHARE. Poverty is deep rooted in this region and bondage to the landlords is entrenched. It will take some time for women to build up their capacity, and their courage, to absorb larger loans and take more charge of their lives. But there are already signs that some are beginning to do this, and they will stand as examples for other women. It may take longer for Veldurti Branch to become viable compared to Dachepally and the staff work under tougher conditions.

But if SHARE can succeed in Veldurti, as well as in the more vibrant economy around the Dachepally Branch, then it can confidently take on all the districts of Andhra Pradesh, which stretch from the lush coastal plain to the dry rocky hills of the west.

Impact on the Poor

Mr R.P. Wijewardena, from the Savecred Project of Redd Barna in Sri Lanka, visited SHARE in April 1994, 11 months after they had disbursed their first loans, to conduct a mid-term evaluation for CASHPOR. He found they had already enrolled 205 women, more than double the projected numbers for the first year. Their disbursement was also more than double the first year projections. He was so impressed by their progress, and the efficiency with which they were implementing the Grameen Bank methodology, that he recommended they should no longer be regarded as a pilot project. SHARE should go immediately to the next phase of scaling up to viability by reaching 1,000 borrowers in their second year, rather than the projected 500, he advised.

Mr Wijewardena was satisfied with the conduct of centre meetings and the careful financial control at the branch offices. He also reported on the way in which women members responded to help the centre at Allugundu, where houses were burned down by a mob.

> Apart from the immediate measures taken by the Managing Director himself and his staff, members from both branches contributed clothes, medicine and food items from their own tiny stock to fulfil the urgent needs of the victims. This is a remarkable exhibition of the social accountability which is an important element expected to be developed by the programme.

Mr Wijiwardena's only major concern about the SHARE project was its high cost. He reported that in its eleventh month, the unit cost of disbursing one rupee was 1.49 rupees, which even in these early days of the project seemed unduly high. He recommended that costs be brought down by expanding to reach at least 1,000 members in the next year 'since SHARE has the capacity to do so' and that earnings be increased by raising the loan size ceiling to Rs3,000 (US$97).

In February 1995, nearly two years after the first loan disbursement, Professor David Gibbons, Executive Trustee of CASHPOR and Helen Todd, Editor of *Credit for the Poor,* spent a week visiting SHARE's head office in Hyderabad and both its branches for the final evaluation required by APDC. As

Raising the House with her own Hands

The combination of daily labour and the new milk income has enabled poor landless women in the Dachepally Branch to make a difference in their households even in their first loan cycles.

In a low-lying area of Veerapuram village, Darmawati sits in front of a battered mud hut. Her husband is chopping firewood in slow motion, sitting down, wheezing loudly with the asthma which has made him unable to work for several years. Darmawati is on her second loan. She bought a Rs3,000 buffalo with her first loan, topping up her SHARE loan with a private loan from a relative, both of which she repaid easily from the milk income. With her second she bought a better buffalo for Rs4,500, this time making up the difference from her savings. She has two calves from these useful beasts and they give her five litres of milk, or Rs40, per day. She has used part of this income to finance the inputs of leasehold land cultivated by her two married sons. She is managing the household income — the profits from the harvest of this land go into her personal account in a bank in town. (SHARE does not have personal savings accounts, so is not yet benefiting from its members' ability to save.) Before the monsoon she is going to spend these savings to raise the houselot and strengthen the house, so that it will be high above the floods that attack it every year.

Anasuya, a 28-year-old woman in the same village who took her first loan nearly a year ago, insists on showing us two houses. One was the house they rented when they came here five years ago, which is now occupied by someone else. The other is the house they proudly bought four months back. She did not buy it directly from her loan. She bought a buffalo, which doubled her daily income. This enabled the couple to pay the water charges necessary to increase their leasehold paddy land from two acres to three. It was the harvest from this that gave them the surplus to buy the house.

For B Esamma, a tribal woman in Tummalacheruvu village, the milk income from her buffalo loan has enabled her to liberate her youngest child from the necessity of earning for the family. Esamma has four children. Her two boys never went to school and have worked in the fields as daily labourers since they were eight years old. Her elder daughter, equally illiterate, was married off at 14. But since Esamma joined SHARE and became the owner of a buffalo she has decided to keep her youngest daughter in school until she finishes secondary level.

of February 1995, SHARE had 280 members in Veldurti Branch and 480 in Dachepally Branch, making a total of 760 members — all of them women. This exceeded considerably the pilot project target of 495 poor female members over two years. However, it seemed less than SHARE's capacity given that it had taken on eight more staff than projected. Disbursement also exceeded projections of Rs828,000 to be disbursed in 538 small loans (average of Rs1,539 or about US$50). Actual disbursement was R1,307,000 disbursed in 727 small loans (averaging Rs1,798 or about US$58).

Generally most of the members of SHARE appeared to be poor, judging from their housing conditions and limited holdings of agricultural land — especially in the Kurnool District. Exceptions seemed to be rare. Like Nirdhan Nepal, however, there was not enough emphasis on motivating the poorest of the poor first when starting work in a new village. Apart from considerations of equity, we know from experience that it is the poorest women who are most faithful in repayment and the most loyal to their centres.

SHARE's eligibility criteria seem unnecessarily high for rural conditions in India. Households with less than Rs15,000 (about US$500) in total assets, or no more than the equivalent of 2 acres (originally 1 acre) of dry land, are eligible to enter the programme. The poorest of the poor in Andhra Pradesh have much less: no agricultural land and less than Rs5,000 in total assets. As they tend to be tied by bonded labour to the landlords or else to be totally dependent upon them for labour opportunities, they may not come forward to form or participate in groups. Indeed their employers are known to discourage them from doing so with all kinds of false rumours. Moreover, many of the poorest of the poor will be members of scheduled castes who may be discouraged from mixing with others. Finally, by excluding certain tribal people, even members of scheduled tribes — because of their tendency to migrate periodically and because of apparently widespread alcoholism among them — SHARE is limiting its impact on some of the poorest groups.

After this was brought to the attention of SHARE's management, it adopted a low household income criterion of Rs250 (US$8) per capita per month, to ensure that new members will be among the poorest.

As of February 1995 there had been no systematic impact evaluation study of SHARE. However, interviews carried out during the field visit were mainly very positive, and suggest solid income gains, particularly in Dachepally Branch and with borrowers who invested in milch buffaloes — 57% of total borrowers there. Impact on borrower income in the Veldurti Branch will have been less as both feeding the buffaloes and selling their milk are more difficult in that region and only 18% of borrowers took loans for milch buffaloes.

SHARE members on their first loans can take a maximum of Rs2,000 (US$65). Most members in the Dachepally Branch add savings or private borrowings to this sum and buy a milch buffalo for around Rs2,500. This kind of buffalo can give two litres of milk per day which they sell at government collection centres for Rs16. This is already equivalent to the woman's daily wage for working in the fields, which they continue to do. What it means, in effect, is that her daily income doubles, without a great increase in her working hours, since all members of the family gather fodder for the buffalo. They usually get a calf within a year and when they are entitled to their second loan, of Rs3,500, they can buy a better buffalo with a higher daily yield.

Almost all the women SHARE members in both branches are rural day labourers, weeding and transplanting paddy and picking cotton and vegetables for the few landlords who own most of the agricultural land. The husbands of most SHARE members are also day labourers — earning Rs25 per day. Therefore, a labouring women earning Rs15 a day, and also pulling in Rs16 a day from the milk of her buffalo, is already, on her first loan, contributing more to the household income than her husband.

The loan size is important. In a credit programme in Tamil Nadu, the next door state to the south, also working with rural women labourers, lack of funds was keeping the loan sizes at around Rs500. These borrowers complained this sum was not enough to buy a buffalo and so they used their loans mostly for emergency consumption — like school fees. With a starting loan of Rs2,000, SHARE's members, at least in the opportunity-rich Dachepally Branch, can immediately buy an income-generating asset. Because these women are already earning through daily labour, the repayments on this loan are not too large for very poor women to manage.

Self-Employment

Inference also enables us to conclude that the impact of SHARE on employment among its beneficiaries has been positive and widespread. As most of the loans seem to have been used by the women borrowers themselves to generate additional self-employment (mainly in animal husbandry: 67% in Dachepally and 70% in Veldurti), they will have been more fully employed or employed in higher value-added activities, because of their investments. In addition, some of the other investments, e.g., cultivation and trading, will have provided additional

---

Buffalo Loans

In the scheduled tribe section of a village in the Dachepally Branch in the Guntur District is a SHARE group who all invested their first loans in milch buffaloes. This is a large village and it is easy to see where the tribal section begins. It is where the brick and tile houses suddenly give way to mud and thatch huts and where the road collapses into yellow dirt. Each woman is keen to tell us why buffaloes are a good investment:

We know how to look after a buffalo and the traditional ways to cure its illnesses. Also there is a veterinary service in the village if we need it. It is common here for a father to give his daughter a buffalo when she marries, that is how we know how to care for them.
The milk is easy to sell at the government milk collection centre. Even if we are too lazy to go there, there are also middlemen buying milk from door to door.
We get a daily income from the milk; better still, we own an asset.
Part of the milk I keep for my children. I make ghee, which I cannot afford to buy, and buttermilk in the summer.

employment for husbands, and a few activities, e.g., shopkeeping, for both wife and husband. The impact of such self-employment must be to lessen the dependence of these poor families on a few landlords who give them daily labour.

As most of the additional income generated by SHARE's loans will have been earned by the women themselves there is a high probability that much of it has been spent on improving the welfare of their households, especially that of the children. Indeed, interviews during the field visit showed that children, including girls, are being kept in school longer as a result of higher household income, and diets are better, partly as a result of some buffalo milk being available. In addition, housing has been improved with the repair or replacement of leaky roofs and walls.

However, a cultural practice that may limit this impact among Hindu households is the tendency for all funds to be kept and managed by the husband. Even in the case of selling the buffalo milk, it is common for the husbands to carry the milk to the collection centres and to receive the payment. The tendency for husbands to spend more than wives on their own pleasures is well known and surely reduces the funds available for improving the socio-economic welfare of poor households.

While there may be little SHARE can do about this in the short term, over time the social position of poor women in their families and the community should improve as their income increases. A woman who begins to earn more regularly than her husband is likely to get a larger role in household decision-making and more control over its budget. Violence against women and their exclusion from household decision-making are likely to be reduced. SHARE should do all it can to encourage this process in its motivation work in the centres.

The High Cost of SHARE

SHARE's operating costs at the time of the final evaluation visit were way beyond its income from interest earned on its loans to the members. For the 10 months from 1 April 1994 to 31 January 1995, SHARE's total operating costs were about Rs800,000 (around US$26,000), whereas its interest income actually received during that period was only Rs53,505 (about US$1,700). The interest income covered only about 7% of operating expenses.

The cost per rupee disbursed had gone down to an average of Rs0.82 in the second 10 months of operation as compared to Rs1.49 during the first year, so efficiency had been somewhat improved. Nevertheless costs were higher than those of most start-up replications.

As repayment (of principal and interest) was perfect, none of the big difference between income and expenditure was due to loan losses. It was a function, therefore, of an inappropriately low interest rate on loans to borrowers, high costs and lower than possible disbursement.

The nominal interest rate being charged to borrowers was 10% per annum. However, as interest was calculated on the principal amount of the loan, although it was repaid weekly over the year-long loan period, the effective interest rate to borrowers was slightly more than 20% per annum. This was a relatively high interest for financial institutions in rural India, which were charging a highly subsidized rate of around 12 to 15% effective per annum. Prudence suggested a higher effective interest rate to enable SHARE to more quickly reach operational self-sufficiency at branch level. The project management had already reached this conclusion for itself, and raised its nominal interest rate to 15% (an effective interest rate to borrowers of just over 30%) as of 1 April 1995. It managed to do this with scarcely a ripple of dissent from its borrowers. So the interest rate was not the culprit.

SHARE's operating costs exceeded its projections in the Project Proposal. Staff costs were projected to average in total about Rs38,000 per month during the second year of operation, but actually they had averaged nearly Rs42,000. Staff travel allowances also had averaged considerably more in the second year of operation than budgeted, over Rs12,200 per month as compared to the Rs7,200 budgeted. Part of this high cost of travel is due to the long distances that the MD and the monitoring staff at Head Office have to travel to the branches, which are respectively 210km and 230km from Hyderabad in opposite directions.

Altogether staff salaries and travel allowances accounted for two-thirds of total operating expenditures, which is about average for GB-type programmes. This means that other expenditures probably were also on the high side compared to the budget projections. For example, office rent and utilities were averaging over Rs5000 per month during the second year of operation as compared to the Rs1,650 budgeted.

Much of SHARE's relatively high staff expenditure was being incurred in laying the foundation for expansion. As of end January 1995, a total of 19 staff were employed by SHARE as compared to the 11 that had been budgeted. Of the 8 non-budgeted staff, 4 were support staff in the Head Office and 4 were trainees in the field. While SHARE was incurring high cost in training new staff, however, it was putting the brakes on both group formation and disbursement, so that the staff it had were underutilized. In its second year, SHARE grew from 205 members to 830, a reasonable result — until one compares it with Nirdhan Nepal, which in the same period grew from 155 members to 1,345. In its second year, SHARE's average loans outstanding were only US$15,213. (Nirdhan Nepal had almost four times as much money out in the hands of the borrowers.)

This, then, is the fundamental reason for SHARE's high unit cost. It was building a professional, well-trained and well-paid Head Office and Branch staff with the capacity to expand the programme; but expansion was slow and this staff was just not getting enough units out to clients. This disappointing rate of growth in both members and loans outstanding continued into SHARE's third year. By March 1996, Nirdhan Nepal had more than 2,500 members, TYM had

2,100 and SHARE had less than 1,500, with a growth of only 8% in that quarter. Loans outstanding were around half of Nirdhan's.

Mr Udaia Kumar points to the 'fund crunch' which caused this slowdown:

> SHARE started with two branches and had to face initial teething problems. Mobilizing financial resources was difficult as the programme was new. External factors were not favourable and the permission from Ministry of Finance and Reserve Bank of India to obtain loans from GT took a lot of time. Funds from APDC were lost in transit...This resulted in a funds crunch and we had to slow down the field operations. As such, the rate of expansion during the initial two/three years slowed down, utilizing only 30-40 per cent capacity of staff members. Discussion for a funding relationship with NABARD, SIDBI, Andhra Pradesh Government and local banks is on, but limited funds have been received as yet. (Letter to CASHPOR, August 1996.)

As Mr Udaia points out, there are particular constraints in the Indian context which make it difficult for NGOs doing Grameen Banking to get funding support, particularly operating funds. Many donors and development agencies working in the Indian context believe in a 'holistic' development strategy and will not fund credit-as-an-entry-point programmes like GBRs. Others have such a strong 'charity' approach that they have rejected SHARE because they consider its interest rate 'too high'. SHARE's legal status as a 'society' makes it virtually impossible to do business with commercial banks, as shall be discussed below. As a result, unlike Nirdhan Nepal, which is now getting most of its funds from commercial sources, SHARE has not yet accessed significant funds from banks.

Given this context, Mr Udaia's financial management has been very cautious. Unless he is fully confident of fund supply, he has tended to keep large amounts on fixed deposit and keep a rein on group formation by his staff. Apart from housing loans in 1996, he had not ventured into special loans alongside the general loan. The result of SHARE's slow expansion is continuing high unit costs and inadequate utilization of its field staff. At end 1995, each of SHARE's seven trained field assistants (excluding trainees) were servicing, on average, 115 borrowers, against an optimum of between 300 to 400, under the Grameen Bank model. This underuse of trained staff is reflected in the high unit cost per dollar disbursed, which by end 1995 was 38 cents, compared to Nirdhan Nepal's 20 cents.

SHARE has the capacity, in its cadre of experienced field and management staff, to expand much more rapidly. It has formulated a plan to scale up to full financial sustainability by opening six new branches, bring its total number of branches to eight. Under this plan, it will reach 20,000 borrowers by the fourth year, at which time all branch costs and 95% of its head office costs will be covered by interest income. Its unit cost will still be higher than other projects, at 34 cents, but its field staff will be stretched, handling an average of 300 clients each. The critical question is how will SHARE get the large amount of funds

Strength of Samson

K. Samson, a 24-year-old trainee project assistant in the Dachepally Branch of SHARE, sits crosslegged on a *charpoy* (a string bed) talking to five potential borrowers who have just formed themselves into a group. He is perfectly at ease, not surprisingly. Any one of these women could be his mother.

Samson comes from a poor family in a nearby subdistrict. Both his father and his mother work as daily labourers, and he remembers the struggle they went through to keep himself and his brother in school. Both the brothers made it through college and Samson got a job as a warden in a residential college, where he was able to pad out his earnings by giving tuition to the students. But he wasn't satisfied. 'I wanted to work in the villages and help the poor. So when I saw the advertisement for this work with SHARE I took it.'

Samson has been a trainee for 11 months and in that time has motivated and trained 21 five-member groups in six villages, more than any other staff member in the Branch.

'This is very satisfying work. I don't find anything difficult. I know the psychology of the people because I grew up like this. This programme is good for women. We organize the centre in the village and the women can choose their own project so that it fits in with their daily labour and their domestic work, while still raising their incomes.'

Like all the other staff in the Dachepally Branch, Samson carries around with him a 'motivation folder' — an imaginative collection of cartoons, diagrams and photographs neatly bound into a book — which he uses to show prospective borrowers what members in other villages are doing with their loans and the basic functions of groups, centres and group fund savings.

He uses it to quiet the natural fears of poor women. 'In one village there was one very poor woman who was frightened to join. She told me: "How can I manage the repayment? If my project loses what will I do?" So I showed her others who were doing well and I explained that the centre will help. Finally, she took the courage to form her own group. Now she is such an enthusiastic member that she has been elected Centre Chief.'

required to carry out these expansion plans.

Finding a Legal Form for Growth

Of the four projects examined in this book, SHARE is undoubtedly the most faithful replication of the Grameen Bank methodology and the best managed programme on the ground. Targeting was a little loose at first, but was tightened up considerably in the second year. Evaluations found few serious problems with credit discipline and loan utilization in the centres. Defaults were zero. Staff were well trained and closely supervised by both branch and head office and SHARE seems to have avoided the crises of staff dishonesty and demoralization which hit some other projects.

Mr Udaia's competence and his promotion of the Grameen model, as well as the success of SHARE, is attracting considerable interest in India and amongst international donors. In 1995, SHARE obtained approval from the Grameen Trust for a plan to scale up the Dachepally Branch to financial viability by early 1997. The Trust agreed to provide US$100,000 in recoverable grant and soft loan for this purpose over two years. The branch in fact covered its operational costs a year ahead of schedule.

Mr Udaia and CASHPOR established a dialogue with NABARD, the National Bank for Agricultural and Rural Development, which showed a keen interest in how the Grameen model was performing in India. This contact resulted in the offer of a line of credit of Rs2,500,000 (about US$80,000) for loan capital to fuel expansion in Kurnool District. (It is not clear why much of this credit line was not utilized.) The state government of Andhra Pradesh is discussing with SHARE its support for an expansion of its operations to serve schedule cast and scheduled tribal groups throughout the state. SHARE has submitted other proposals for operational support to NABARD, HUDCO and SIDBI. SHELTER, another international donor, is providing finance for housing loans — and 256 loans amounting to US$67,352 had been disbursed by May 1996.

To establish six new branches, thereby bringing its total to the eight required for organizational viability, and to bring all the branches to financial viability themselves, SHARE estimates it will need financing of about US$900,000. To reach all of the 2.5 million poor households in Andhra Pradesh that could benefit from its loans, SHARE would need around US$200 million, most of it, of course, in on-lending funds. Most of such funds would have to come from domestic banks. Whether SHARE will be able to access such funds probably depends on its finding a legal status and an institutional form to which banks will lend.

Institutionalization

SHARE is registered under the Societies Act and under FCRA which enables it to receive grants from foreign sources. In addition, it got permission from the Ministry of Finance of the Government of India, and Reserve Bank of India to receive two soft loans from the Grameen Trust. Under the Societies Act, SHARE can do limited banking with its members — that is, disbursing loans and mobilizing savings. The Reserve Bank of India non-banking finance company guidelines do not apply. (Nagarajan PBT Association Inc., 1995:Vol 2, pp 9-10).

The 'looseness' of the Societies framework has been a useful vehicle for SHARE to commence operations and to adapt the Grameen Bank methodology to Andhra Pradesh conditions. But the position of a society is not suitable for a microfinance institution in the long term, as Mr Udaia points out:

> Societies/Trusts are considered as non-business associations or charitable institutions. Scaling up operations and reaching out to larger numbers of rural poor becomes difficult because of   1) restrictions on savings deposits   2) banks are reluctant to provide revolving loan funds to societies which cannot raise equity 3) dividends cannot be disbursed and equity cannot be serviced   4) borrowers cannot be part of the Governing Body as the Income Tax Act does not permit the members to derive any direct or indirect benefits from the funds of the Society.

SHARE has already discovered that banks will not lend the large sums required for expansion to a society which is not required to have any capital and which is not regulated by the Reserve Bank of India.

Of course, not only SHARE, but all NGOs in India that are carrying out financial intermediation with the poor are in this situation with respect to the lack of supervision of their fiduciary relationship with their depositors. While this is almost certainly beneficial to all concerned at this early, still experimental, stage in the development of financial institutions for the poor, it is not a sound basis for their expansion and institutionalization.

In May 1996, the newly-formed INDNET — the National Network of Grameen Bank Replicators in India — led by SHARE and ASA, held a workshop to consider this problem of finding the right institutional form for microfinance institutions. At the end of the workshop three of the participants, including SHARE, decided to institutionalize their credit programmes into Non-Banking Financial Institutions under the Companies Act. Although the workshop was warned that running an NBFI required 'organizational sophistication', its advantages in doing large-scale and high volume savings mobilization and loan disbursement make it suitable for GBRs wanting to expand. An NBFI can mobilize share capital, borrow funds from banks and retail credit after retaining its own margins. Its depositors are protected under regulations from the Reserve Bank of India. However, the Reserve Bank puts a cap on interest rates (currently 15%) and deposits are limited to a factor of two times its net owned funds. Perhaps the next step for INDNET is to lobby the government of India to remove interest caps which make it impossible for microfinance institutions to become self-sustaining.

Grabbing The Second Chance

Sanjamma spent most of her youth trying to get an education, but poverty finally defeated her. Now she is putting the same determination into a tailoring business with much more hope of success. As a young girl she went to school in Amadaguntla, where her father was a cobbler with some land. But kin conflict and illness forced the family to sell everything and take refuge in Bommireddipally village, 6km. from Veldurti, as squatters on the houselot of her mother's sister. Their poverty and the illness of herself and both her parents, meant that Sanjamma could not go back to school.

When she got better and in the teeth of family opposition, Sanjamma went to stay with a cousin in Dhone so that she could enrol in a school there. But there simply was not enough money for her expenses and problems in her cousin's house finally forced her back to the life of hopelessness at home. Sanjamma couldn't stand it. In her teens she ran away to an *ashram* for destitutes in Bellary in the state of Karnataka. There she found a little peace and rest, and learned to be a skilled tailor.

Everything was going her way. She met Christopher, a bus conductor, and married him without informing their parents. They settled happily in his village and he helped her to study privately for the 10th class examination. Sadly, she failed. Gradually her in-laws began to pressure her for dowry and finally, in fear of her life, she fled Karnataka and returned to her parent's.

Christopher remarried and got his dowry, but he continued to visit Sanjamma regularly and two children were born. Sanjamma kept them through daily labour, but it looked as though their lives would simply repeat the deprivation and frustration of her own.

When SHARE staff appeared in Bommireddipally, Sanjamma did not wait for them to come to her. She went to them and asked them to help her form a group. Her parents were afraid and predicted another disaster, but Sanjamma walked boldly to the group training sessions and learned quickly. In June, 1993, she got her loan of Rs1,500 and bought a sewing machine.

Sanjamma had learned modern designs in Karnataka and she soon established herself as a popular tailor. Her weekly earnings are between Rs100 to Rs120 per week, and before festive seasons she pulls in up to Rs500 a week. Repayment of Rs33 weekly to SHARE is not a problem. Sanjamma still does daily labour and fulfils her orders at night — for which she has connected electricity to her parent's house. Her plan now is to buy a plot of land and build her own house. With her second loan she aims to buy a milk cow or a buffalo, which should double her daily income.

Sanjamma is a transformed woman, with confidence and enthusiasm. This time, she belives she has a bright future ahead and she trusts that SHARE will bring happiness to many more women blocked by poverty.

Case study condensed from Annual Report, April 1993-March 1994

3

Nirdhan, West Bengal

MD. RASHIDULL ALAM AND ABDUS SALAM KHAN

PROJECT NIRDHAN, WEST BENGAL, began operations in Palla Road, Burdwan District, 150km from Calcutta in mid-1993. Its founder, Professor Jayanta Kumar Ray, knew the Grameen Bank well, having written one of the first books on the Bank and its impact on poor women borrowers.[1] The project was implemented through the South Asia Research Society (SARS), an NGO registered under the Societies Act, of which Professor Ray is the President.

In his concept proposal for funding to APDC, Professor Ray announced that he wished to test a 'refinement of the Grameen Bank model' which would include group enterprises to spread the benefits of the credit programme out to other poor families who may not be enterprising enough to join the programme directly. Also, to counter criticisms that Grameen Bank clients remain dependent on the Bank, Professor Ray thought it was important to 'integrate health, education, non-farm employment, farming and agro-industry, so... as to generate capabilities for long-term self-reliance...'[2]

During the early implementation of the project, the management staff quickly ran up against a very powerful political élite entrenched in the villages who were highly suspicious of their efforts to mobilize the poor. No field staff were appointed during the first six months of project operation. To insulate themselves from this hostile élite and their potentially violent opposition to the programme, Nirdhan decided to work through 'volunteers' and 'facilitators' — politically acceptable local men helping on a voluntary basis — who played a large role in the early recruitment of members and even in the training of groups.

Professor Ray, who is Centenary Professor of International Relations at the University of Calcutta, was unable, because of his academic commitments and his health, to take on the executive leadership of Nirdhan. He appointed a Project Director, a Project Manager and two branch managers, and all four were sent for training with AIM, Malaysia, funded by APDC, and then to the Grameen Bank funded by the Grameen Trust, before operations began. However, within a year only one of these trained officers remained. One branch manager was dismissed for being absent from his branch for long periods without excuse and both the project director and the project manager resigned. The upheaval caused by this loss of trained staff reverberates through Nirdhan to this day. The SARS Board became disillusioned with what Professor Ray termed 'city-bred officers [who] tend to look for alternative or supplementary occupations, spending a lot of their time away from the villages...'[3] and did not recruit graduate replacements. By the end of 1994 the work on the ground was being done by four 'trainee assistants' — temporary staff recruited in the village and paid very low salaries; only one of the three branches had a branch manager.

Partly by design then, and partly as a response to initial problems of working in the village and of the loss of trained staff, Project Nirdhan became a project which differed in fundamental ways from the Grameen Bank model — its focus was broader than credit and its field operations were dependent on volunteers and on temporary, untrained staff. Rather than sidestep the local power structure, it attempted to conciliate it by working through local notables as 'facilitators'. In addition, it was not geared, like the other projects funded by APDC, towards reaching branch viability through expansion to adequate numbers of borrowers. Instead it aimed to generate income through investment in joint agricultural ventures with borrowers.

In terms of leadership, Nirdhan was also quite different from the three other replications featured in this book. Its founder was knowledgable about Grameen and commited to the project; but was unable to take executive responsibility for making it work. The project director who was hired turned out to be just a 'hiree'. Despite his training at AIM and Grameen Bank, he had so little commitment to Nirdhan that he spent much of his time in Calcutta, 150km from his office at Palla Road, looking for more congenial employment.[4]

Innovations and Deviations

At the end of March 1994, Mr R. P. Wijiwardena of Savecred in Sri Lanka, visited Nirdhan West Bengal to conduct the mid-term assessment for CASHPOR. He was impressed by the way Nirdhan was reaching the poorest women. After less than one year of operation Nirdhan had reached 145 members in eight centres. This exceeded the target of 100 members for the first year. Disbursement was also well ahead of target, with US$5,316 out in the hands of the borrowers. Repayment was an encouraging 100%.

By the time of Mr Wijiwardena's visit, Nirdhan had established two more branches, one in Mogra, 100km from Calcutta in the Hoogly District and the third in the very remote area of Hasnabad, in North 24 Parganas District. While the first branch at Palla Road was stagnating because of the indifference of its staff, Mogra was making quite rapid progress. At Hasnabad, seven male groups had quickly formed themselves into one centre and entered into a joint venture with Nirdhan to set up a prawn-rearing project. Each of the members had

In a Poor State

Project Nirdhan operates in three districts of West Bengal in India. Most communities identified as in the target group belong to the scheduled castes and tribal people or the extreme poor. Some of them are migrants from Bangladesh. A majority of them remain landless and illiterate and they live below the poverty line. Their awareness of the basic rules of health and sanitation is pathetically low.

Housing facilities are extremely poor and most families live in mud huts with thatch roofs. Some people have got government housing. In the village, most people are not using sanitary toilets. They have little knowledge of nutrition and sanitation. The majority of the poor men work as daily labourers on the farms of the landed. Some poor women also work as agricultural labourers, although this is regarded as shameful.

Despite several decades of communist government in West Bengal and large sums of public money put into the co-operative movement, credit is not available to the poor in these villages. In fact, we observed no organization working for the landless poor. When poor families need capital they must borrow from moneylenders, who charge a rate of 2 to 4% interest per month.

Due to their culture, landless women remain confined within their houses. They have very little opportunity to participate in any activity that helps to increase the income of their families. As a result, they are considered as liabilities from an economic point of view.

The aim of Project Nirdhan is to bring about a change in this traditional attitude of society towards women by raising their social status through making them effective earning members of their families.

When women get the credit, they put it into activities they can do at home, like livestock or making puffed rice. Some have traditional skills, like making handlooms (*sana).*

borrowed Rs2,000 (US$65), making a total of Rs70,000 which they collectively invested in the prawn farm. This meant that the average loan outstanding at Hasnabad was nearly three times the average loan of Rs775 (US$25) of the other two branches.

Mr Wijiwardena was not happy with this development. He warned that such large-scale joint ventures should be viewed with 'great care and caution'. He advised that these ambitions should be postponed at least until Nirdhan had reached 1,000 borrowers and had attained 'a reasonable degree of economic viability'.[5]

He was equally disturbed at the presence of the 'facilitators'. He pointed out that the quality of work depends on trained staff and that the presence of these 'alien elements...is likely to affect or even diminish the influence of centre chiefs as it is actually they who should be depended upon to preserve and protect the project...'

His most important recommendations, however, concerned the employment — and deployment — of staff. He noted that the four field assistants had only temporary status and were very poorly paid — on average Rs640 (US$21) a month, compared to the Rs2,500 (US$81) originally budgeted for each field staff. They received no travel allowance and the few bicycles owned by the project were not enough for their needs. Considering their heavy workload and their expected output in the future, he advised that their salaries and allowances be improved.

On the other hand, he thought that generally the management-level staff (the ones who were adequately paid!) were doing very little work. Palla Road in particular was overstaffed and had not formed a new group for several months. He suggested that periodic performance evaluations should be introduced 'to deal appropriately with excesses and shortages in staffing, while ensuring the creation of a disciplined work environment'.

He noted that the Nirdhan management were taking a short cut to financial viability through their investment in joint ventures. They hoped to make a profit of more than Rs200,000 from the Hasnabad prawn project, for example. Mr Wijewardena suggested that the slower route of extending outreach to more members was a safer method. He also warned that the plans to add health and adult literacy programmes to the credit programme should be reconsidered — at least they should be implemented by a different set of staff so as not to distract from the credit delivery.

When this report reached CASHPOR and APDC, it rang alarm bells. The head of APDC wrote to Professor Ray:

> ...the Grameen approach requires rigorously trained, specialized field staff. It cannot depend on part-time, voluntary field staff. In this important respect, Project Nirdhan seems not to have fully implemented the first objective of the pilot project...Apparently, Rs70,000 has already been invested in a prawn joint venture, although this was not envisaged in the project proposal. The Grameen

Bank's experience with joint ventures amongst its borrowers was that generally they failed due to poor managment, and it has severely curtailed loans for this purpose. So Nirdhan's engagement in these joint ventures is dangerous and should be discouraged.[6]

CASHPOR advised that the second tranche of funds be withheld until Professor Ray took on the executive direction of Nirdhan himself and promised to retain/recruit and train six full-time, adequately paid field staff and one branch manager — the only way in which it could build the training capacity to expand.

Professor Ray agreed to these conditions and promised to return to the straight and narrow road of credit delivery. The second tranche of funds was released.

In response to the mid-term evaluation report and APDC's demands, Nirdhan West Bengal did make some important policy changes. There were no more joint ventures. The prawn project failed and all of the 35 male members who had put their first loans into it dropped out of the programme. Ambitious plans to widen the scope of the programme into social welfare activities, like health and literacy, were put on the back burner.

Professor Ray did not take on the executive management of Nirdhan. However, he persuaded the General Secretary of SARS, Mr. Dwijendra Kumar Sen Gupta, a very senior retired officer from the State Bank of India, to take over as *de facto* executive director. In 1995 a trainee branch manager was appointed to Hasnabad, and soon very impressive results in terms of group formation were coming out of this very poor and inaccessible area.

On the question of staffing, however, Professor Ray was adamant that in the conditions of West Bengal, his recruitment policy was the best option.

One effective way...to counteract the resistance of local politicians is to recruit some (not all) bank workers from relevant localities. Their formal educational qualifications are not high, nor are their economic demands. With some training in the GBFS, they have proved themselves to be honest and dedicated replicators.

The use of such terms as 'Trainee Assistants' is an innovative response to the long-prevalent situation in West Bengal, where negative trade unionism (backed by mindless judicial intervention) has destroyed many excellent NGOs. These terms carry a legal safeguard which we can discard only at our peril.

As a result, the remuneration of staff was improved somewhat, but they remained employed on a temporary basis, without travel or other allowances. As the final evaluation was to reveal, no systematic training was offered to these field staff. Grameen Bank practice, which is to assign field staff outside their home villages in order to avoid the social pressures that press on them through family members, was ignored.

Grameen Bankers Give Advice

Strong feelings were aroused by the findings of the first evaluation and the conditions exacted by APDC (on CASHPOR's advice) for releasing the second tranche of funds. In the wake of this CASHPOR decided to ask the Grameen Bank to select a senior officer to visit the project for the final evaluation at the end of the two-year pilot phase. CASHPOR felt that both the experience of a Grameen Banker, and the common language of Bengali, would ease both the giving and the receiving of advice. In the event, two officers, both with long experience as Area and then Zonal managers with the Bank and currently in senior positions in the Grameen Bank Training Institute, went to Nirdhan West Bengal for a month. These officers interviewed many borrowers in the Palla Road and Mogra branches, followed the staff in all their field work and went through the project accounts with a fine comb. No replication has ever had this kind of sustained attention from such experienced Grameen Bankers. Their report is a mass of detailed commentary, focusing on the functioning of the centres in the village and the financial management of the branch. Despite its length, it is reproduced in full in this chapter, because of the value of this commentary for all other Grameen Bank replicators.

Although it is critical of Nirdhan at many points, most of the problems discussed are those which confront new replications and the recommendations are of value to all projects trying to upgrade the professionalism of their staff.

Final Evaluation Report
by Md. Rashidull Alam and Abdus Salam Khan

Nirdhan's greatest strength is its operation in an area of quite desperate poverty and need. The women who have joined the Nirdhan centres have never been offered this kind of opportunity before. So it is their sincerity and commitment, and the small size of their loans, that are the basis of the 100% repayment rate and their loyalty to their centres.

The Nirdhan staff have succeeded in targeting the poorest in the villages and there has been very little leakage to the non-poor. Even more encouraging, when we interviewed 25 second-time borrowers in depth we found that 19 of them had managed to improve their income and social status considerably.

However, we observed that centre members are not well informed about their roles and responsibilities, centre meetings are quite disorganized and there is confusion about matters like the Group Tax. This indicates some weakness in the group training as well as inadequate field supervision by the branch staff. Perhaps the low salary received by the field staff (compared to the national pay scale) combined with lack of job security is responsible for their lack of interest.

We noticed a lack of administrative control and guidance from the Head

Office to the branches. Similarly, there is very little systematic information coming up from the branches to the Head Office. As a result, nobody really knows what is going on in the field.

The cost of the Nirdhan operation is still very high and staff are seriously under-utilized. At the branch, there is no plan and budget by which staff can measure their progress because there are no targets for the branch manager or the staff members to fulfil. What we have tried to do in the following report is to describe the strengths and weaknesses in the field work, the keeping of accounts, the fund management and the monitoring system and give our advice as to how these systems can be improved to bring them up to the standard of systems used in the Grameen Bank.

Group Formation

At the time of our visit we asked the branch staff what are their criteria for group formation. They replied that though they have no written criteria, in practice they follow the Grameen Bank (GB) criteria of group formation. (These are ownership of less than half an acre of agricultural land and assets of less than the value of one acre. Ed.)

We visited the houses of 298 members in both branches to check the quality of group formation. Out of this number, 29 members (10%) were not bottom poor. By the GB criteria they are not eligible to join the project. This is, however, not a large amount of leakage to the non-poor.

By the GB criteria it is not desirable to form a group with close relatives (as for example mother, sister, aunt, mother-in-law etc.). But we observed in Mogra branch that there were some close relatives in the same groups.

A lack of group feeling and close relationship was observed in some centres. We found at Centre no 4 in Palla Road branch that there was amongst the borrowers no mutual understanding and no mutual co-operation. For this reason the same centre meeting was held at two places on the same day. This indicates weak group formation.

We discovered that in most villages the Nirdhan staff have a so-called 'Facilitator' who is supposed to help without remuneration. At the initial stage of group formation, the field assistant depends on these 'Facilitators' to reach the villagers and sometimes they conduct the group training. We feel that this may be one of the reasons for weak group formation.

The monthly average group formation rate of both branches is very low (1.4 in Palla Road and 2 in Mogra).

Group Training

After the formation of a group, members are obliged to participate in compulsory group training. Although the minimum group training period is seven days, it can

---

Another Chit Fund? Nirdhan Convinces Critics

Initially a lot of labour-intensive and extended contact was needed to form groups among the poor women. While these groups were being formed and then trained, staff and the group members had to face all kinds of criticism, false propaganda and irritating, sarcastic remarks from other villagers.

People thought that Project Nirdhan was just another chit fund agent, out to cheat innocent villagers as so many times in the past. But the few group members who did the first training were so motivated that they ignored all these remarks. They were firm to attend their centre meetings so that they could all get their first loans. Then as they gained confidence and organizational strength they were able to win over most of the menfolk who had been so critical.

These women paved the way to form new groups with less trouble and opposition. Regular centre meetings and the open transaction of all business at the meetings raised the confidence of people in the village towards Project Nirdhan. In areas where Nirdhan has been in operation for a year or more, people are more and more interested in joining and faithful in their attendance at the training sessions.

Even the local co-operative leaders and *panchayat prabhans* (local self-government authorities) who were initially indifferent or hostile, became curious enough to attend the centre meetings and went away very impressed at seeing how disciplined and businesslike the women were in conducting their meetings. They could hardly believe their eyes seeing poor women regularly saving, repaying their loans 100% and translating the 'Ten Decisions' into action. They commented that Nirdhan members are more participative than the members of co-operatives.

Professor Jayanta Kumar Ray, Final Project Report

---

go on until the group passes the group recognition test. This training programme is conducted by the Field Assistant (FA). However, sometimes in Nirdhan this training is conducted by one of the 'Facilitators'. The contents of this group training are the duties and responsibilities of group members, group chairpersons and Centre Chiefs, the procedures of loan disbursement and repayment, the group fund, loan utilization and the 10 decisions. Each group member must contribute Rs10 as a training charge, which goes into a newly-opened group fund. We were not able to observe this training because at the time of our visit no groups were being trained. But from what we could gather from interviewing the members, overall group training is not satisfactory. It is clear that compulsory group training has not been conducted properly by the FA. We questioned members about Nirdhan rules and regulations at the time of our centre meeting visit and few members could give satisfactory replies.

Nirdhan's social programme is encapsulated in the 10 Decisions, which should be well known by all members. But none of the members we asked could remember the 10 Decisions. This indicates a lack of proper group training.

Group Recognition Test (GRT)

According to Nirdhan's project proposal, trained groups would be tested by a head office representative. We did not observe any GRT. We asked the members and field assistants who recognized the groups. They replied that normally the General Secretary (who performs the role of project Director) recognizes the group. In the absence of the General Secretary, the Branch Manager recognizes the group. A member of the *panchayat* (representative of the local government) may attend the GRT as an observer.

The Nirdhan project does not have the practice of filling a personal bio-data form (membership form) before the group recognition test. This acts as a record of their income and assets to make sure they are in the target group, and is the base line for later evaluations of the impact of the programme.

Whether the group is recognized or not they are not given any official document. Nirdhan does not maintain a master group register. In Palla Road Branch, we observed 15 group members receiving loans but whether they were recognized or not was not clear to us, because their membership forms are not approved by either the Branch Manager or the General Secretary.

Centre Discipline

Centre Meeting

In the Nirdhan project the weekly centre meeting is held from the next week after Group recognition. Every branch has a centre meeting schedule. Every FA usually attends the centre meeting as scheduled. Every member assembles in the centre before the field assistant arrives. During the meeting current issues of interest to the members are discussed, various problems are raised, repayment of loans and other project business is conducted.

We visited many centre meetings in both branches. We observed that most FAs reached the centre meeting punctually, but a few were up to 10 or 20 minutes late.

The centre meeting starts when the FA arrives. However, nobody formally starts the centre meeting, as is the practice in the Grameen Bank. The group chairpersons collect the pass-books and instalments from all of her group members and give these to the Centre Chief, who submits them to the FA.

In the centre meeting we observed some irregularities, as follows:

- In both branches, all the centre meetings are held between 2 p.m. and 6 p.m. This timing of the centre meetings causes many problems. It is more difficult for the FA to travel in the heat of the early afternoon and this is also the time of monsoon storms. It means that the collection cannot be banked on the same day and the branch office is forced to hold too much cash in hand. This raises the dangers of appropriation, by robbery or by corrupt staff. Afternoon meetings restrict the capacity of the staff to check the utilization of loans and conduct motivation work and compulsory group training. Members also face problems in reaching their homes before dark. According to the General Secretary these meetings have been fixed in the afternoon at the request of the members, because many of them leave early in the morning for daily labour.
- There are no Centre houses, except one in the Mogra branch. Centre meetings are held in the compound of a member's house or in the corridor of their house. These places are not suitable for centre meetings.
- The Group members sit one behind the other instead of in rows, Grameen-style. This means that group members cannot make face to face contact with each other. The group chairpersons and the secretaries do not sit in fixed places.

These weaknesses result in disorganized centre meetings and ultimately affect the discipline which is so very essential in this system of credit operation.

Attendance at the Centre Meetings

It is compulsory for every Nirdhan member to attend the weekly centre meeting. We visited five centre meetings (out of seven) in Palla Road branch and nine centre meetings (out of 13) in Mogra branch. We observed most members attended the centre meeting at the scheduled time. At the time of our visit the average attendance rate at centre meetings was 88%. All the centres maintained an attendance register.

At the centre meetings we observed some irregularities, such as centres 3,4,and 6 in Palla Road branch and centres 8 and 11 in Mogra branch, did not hold their meetings at the scheduled time. After our arrival at the centre meeting, members trickled in one after another. Some came only when the meeting was almost over. The group chairpersons, Centre Chief and FA did not take any action against the late comers. Here there is scope for improvement.

Credit Delivery; Credit Discipline

Loan Proposal

Loan proposals are made at the centre on the prescribed loan proposal form. If the Group Chairperson and Centre Chief agree with the proposal then the Centre

Chillies and Sweet Water Build a Centre House

Lakshmi, who was eight months pregnant, did not feel well on the morning of the centre meeting, but she was determined to go. One of her group members was submitting her loan application and what if Lakshmi's absence meant it could not be approved? But towards the end of the meeting Lakshmi's labour pains began full and strong. The centre members, without waiting for the help or permission of the village men, who were out working in the fields, decided to carry Lakshmi themselves on foot to the nearest health centre. This was 12 kilometres away and they had to cross two rivers. But they made it in time, Lakshmi had her baby safely, and was soon happily back at home.

At another centre at Kothabari, in the Hasnabad branch, the forty members decided to lease a one acre plot of land to grow chillies. They all combined to do the work after they had returned from their daily labour. When the plot needed watering they formed a long line from the pond and passed the buckets of sweet water along in relays. When the chillies were ripe they sold them and used the profit to build their centre house, which now stands as a solid symbol of their joint effort and commitment.

The Nirdhan staff report a growing number of incidents which show members becoming more conscious of their obligations to fellow group and centre members and loyalty to their centres. Members have been willing to help out with the repayment of others who are seriously ill. Some centres have used their combined pressure to stop the drinking of country liquor in their villages. Others have taken their children *en masse* to the health centres to get the oral polio vaccination on the dates fixed by the government.

'These actions show us that Nirdhan has not only succeeded in raising the economic status of our members, but also helped develop their self-respect and self-confidence,' Professor Ray writes.

Source: Final Project Report, Feb. 1996

Chief submits it to the FA. If satisfactory, then the FA sends it to the Branch Manager for final approval. In the prescribed loan proposal form there is no column for the FA and Branch Manager to reduce the amount of loan.

Loan Approval

In the project proposal of Nirdhan, loan proposals should be approved by the Head Office. But in practice the Branch Manager approved all loan proposals of up to Rs1,000 per member. This is actually a violation of GBFS. We also found in both branches some loans disbursed without the approval of either Head

Office or the Branch Manager. When we asked the General Secretary of Nirdhan about this irregularity he explained that in Mogra branch at that time the Branch Manager was absent so the FA received the General Secretary's oral permission to disburse the loan. He was not aware of the instances of irregular loan disbursal in the Palla Road branch.

Loan Disbursement

According to Nirdhan procedure, loan disbursement is made at the centre meeting. They have two types of loans, General and Seasonal. After completion of weekly collection the Field Assistant hands over the loan amount to the Centre Chief, and the Centre Chief disburses, the loan to the member. The Branch Manager's presence is not necessary. The Branch Manager explained that if they disbursed the loans at the branch office the members involved would lose one day's labour and would have to pay so many rupees for transport.

We feel that if the loan disbursement is conducted at the centre, the following problems may arise. The Field Assistant can abscond with the money or be robbed on the way to the meeting. The Branch Manager does not meet the borrowers and his importance in the eyes of the members may decline. Loan disbursement can only be made on the day of the centre meeting and so the loan disbursement cannot be spread evenly through the week.

Loan Utilization

In the Nirdhan project we have observed that most borrowers utilize their loans properly. In both branches 219 borrowers were questioned about their loan utilization. Most spent their loans on paddy husking, cow fattening, goat purchase, pig fattening, and bullock raising. Out of 219 borrowers, 149 (68%) had used their loans properly and 70 (32%) had not used their loans for the stated purpose. Most women borrowers were using their loans themselves.

It was further found that out of 211 borrowers, 34 (16%) were making high profit, 141 (67%) were making moderate profits and 36 (17%) had lost their capital.

Loan Repayment

The loan repayment rate of both branches is satisfactory. We examined the current and previous seven-week recovery rate. It was found to be 100%. We observed that the small size of the individual loans combined with the sincerity and commitment of the borrowers are the principal factors behind this high rate of repayment.

Group Fund

In the Nirdhan project, as in the Grameen Bank, every group has a group fund. Although its composition is the same as in Grameen Bank, and every week group members add to it their compulsory savings of Rs100, the way the group fund is administered is completely different from GBFS. These differences cause a loss of earnings to the project. The group fund is not being used to build the unity and joint responsibility of the group.

Accounting System of Group Fund

The branch office opens a group fund account in a commercial bank. All the group fund savings are daily deposited in that account. Savings in the centre fund are also deposited in the group fund account. The branch office does not open a Group Fund Account in their branch. When members need a group fund loan then the branch office requests Head Office to send a cheque for withdrawal of the amount.

The Branch office does not maintain a Group-Fund ledger nor do group members have Group Fund pass-books. In the collection sheet, loan ledger and members' general loan pass-books the project staff simply draw an extra column and note the savings of each individual member.

The commercial bank offers 6% interest on these group fund savings. This interest is credited to that account. Nirdhan does not show group fund savings as their liability and they keep group fund savings completely separate from their book of accounts. We observed in both branches a large amount of group fund savings are deposited in the commercial bank. It would be better fund management to deposit these savings in their own account. Then these funds could be invested at the 10% rate of interest among the members. Since the branch pays 6% on these savings but loans them out at 10%, they can earn a marginal profit of 4%. The General Secretary explained that they could not open a group fund account in the branch because the organization is registered under the Societies Act. According to this Act, they cannot use members' savings.

Group Fund Loan Disbursement

Group fund loans are not disbursed according to a prescribed form. Group loan applications are not signed by the other members of the group. The group fund is being used as individual savings and not to build the unity and responsibility of the group.

Group Tax One

Members contribute 5% of the loan amount to the group fund. The General Secretary informed us that Group Tax One is not refundable. But when we asked the members of Mogra branch whether the Group Tax One is refundable or not, all the members replied that it is refundable if they leave the group. The FA said that they are not clear about what happens to this tax. So it is a matter of confusion.

Field Supervision

Field supervision is a vital function in a credit programme like Nirdhan, because all project activities are implemented through the branch at the centre level. It is essential for the supervising authority to know what is happening at the centre level.

As far as we could discover, the Branch Manager and FA visit the member's houses only at the time of group formation and occasionally after the centre meeting. They do not visit for loan utilization checks. The General Secretary, who holds the supervisory authority over all three branches, visits the centres very rarely. We think that there is considerable scope for improvement in field supervision.

Office Management

At the branch level there is no scheduled office time. The office has no proper filing system and there is no regular correspondence between head office and the branch. We observed a lack of administrative control from the Head Office over the branch. Similarly the HO has so far failed to provide proper instruction and guidance to the field staff.

Staff Training and Performance Measurement

Nirdhan has no real staff training system. We observed that the staff have very little knowledge about the Grameen Bank methodology. After joining the project, trainee managers and FAs go straight to work 'learning by doing'. Sometimes the General Secretary visits the branch and arranges a staff meeting where he discusses with trainee staff about the Grameen approach. But this discussion is not sufficient to develop a professional staff.

At the initial stage of the project SARS sent a team of four staff members to Grameen Bank in Bangladesh and to AIM in Malaysia to study the financial management system geared to delivery and recovery of credit. But after a short time three of them left this project.

Staff Utilization

The Branch Manager should always plan for 100% utilization of staff in his area. He should try to ensure that the output of the branch is maximized with the minimum number of staff. In the Nirdhan project plan each centre should have six groups and each field assistant should handle ten centres. So a fully utilized FA is servicing 60 groups, or 300 members. At the time of our visit utilization of staff was very low — only 30% of capacity in the Palla Road branch (or an average of 90 members per field staff member) and 23% of capacity in the Mogra Branch (or an average of 69 members per field staff member).

Staff Remuneration

Nirdhan has no fixed salary structure. It seems that remuneration of staff is inadequate. We asked the FA about their remuneration and they replied that though at the present time they are not satisfied with their salary, they hope in future it will be increased. They also said they are very satisfied with their present job because they have scope to serve the bottom poor and to show their own creativity.

All the staff are temporary. They get no additional benefits apart from their salary.

Accounting and Financial System

The Nirdhan project has no accounting manual and the branch offices maintain their accounts following head office instructions. In many ways the method of keeping accounts is contrary to the GBFS. Practices which are likely to lead to problems within centres and with the field staff are as follows:

- They do not use a collection sheet at the centre meeting. When we visited the centre meetings it was difficult to identify how much instalment was due and what had been collected.
- They do not maintain a group fund pass-book or a centre fund pass-book.
- There is no evidence of who collects instalments because there is no record when cash passes from one hand to the other.
- Borrowers' pass-books are not reconciled with the loan ledger by the FA.
- Although the branch maintains the cash book and general ledger but it is not signed by anybody in the branch.
- In the absence of the branch manager the collection amounts are put in the cashbox by the FA with their own hands. The cash-book is not updated. The vault register is not maintained.

Fund Management

A serious lack of control has been observed in respect of fund management in both branches.

Idle Funds in the Branches

We observed in Palla Road Branch that nearly Rs36,000 is recorded as cash in hand from October 1994 to June 1995. But this amount was not in the cash box. It was in the hands of the Branch Manager. It was not shown in the daily cash book or the vault register. Neither the Branch Manager nor the General Secretary could give a satisfactory explanation of why this money was not deposited in a commercial bank.

From October 1994 to June 1995 Nirdhan kept an average of Rs15,000 in the commercial bank. These funds (36,000+15,000)=Rs51,000 were completely idle. If they had used these funds properly they could have earned a profit of more than Rs350 per month.

In Mogra branch, there are also large amounts of idle funds in the commercial bank as well as in cash in hand at the branch office. Actual daily amounts in the commercial bank in June ranged from Rs19,900 to Rs31,389, or an average of Rs25,644. The amounts of cash in hand ranged from Rs1,860 to Rs7,461. The group fund balance in the commercial bank ranged from Rs25,043 to Rs27,198, or an average of Rs26,102. If these funds were properly utilized, they could earn a profit in the month of about Rs208.

Operating Costs

We observed the disbursement cost per unit in both branches. In 1994, it cost the Palla Road branch Rs0.41 to disburse one rupee. Their income per unit is Rs0.10, so the net loss is Rs0.31 per unit. Similarly, it cost the Mogra branch Rs0.40 to disburse one rupee, and their net loss per unit is Rs0.30. Unfortunately, because of a decline in disbursement in mid-1995, the disbursement cost per unit was actually rising at the time of our visit.

Monitoring System

The General Secretary holds a staff meeting each month at each branch to review progress and discuss problems. The head office accountant visits each branch each week to check entries in the cash book, general ledger, loan ledger, and other financial documents. In addition, a monthly progress report in a prescribed format is submitted to the head office by the branches.

The weakness of this system is what is *not* reported. Neither arrears nor attendance is reported, so it is not possible to monitor a breakdown of discipline at the centre. The position of cash in hand is also not reported. The branch does not submit weekly, quarterly, half-yearly and yearly statements for comparative monitoring and planning.

Socio-Economic Impact on the Borrowers

Twenty-five borrowers from the two branches were interviewed about the impact of the project on their income and socio-economic welfare. These borrowers were on their second loans.

- Out of 25 borrowers, 19 (76%) borrowers reported that the economic condition of their family had improved. Only 6 borrowers (24%) reported that their economic condition had not improved.
- 21 borrowers (84%) reported that they were more respected in their families after they became active in income-earning activities.
- 18 borrowers (72%) expressed a positive attitude towards family planning. The rest were negative.

- 18 borrowers (72%) thought that they were eating better food. Others saw not much change.

It is our observation that the socio-economic status of the borrowers has improved considerably.

Prospects for Viability

At the time of our visit, neither branch had a plan for expansion nor any projected budget for expenditure. Unless there are some drastic changes of direction we think it is unlikely that Nirdhan can proceed towards viability.

To achieve viability at branch level, a branch must reach full capacity in terms of the number of groups. Within three years a branch should try to form approximately 500 groups. But in two years the total number of groups in the two Nirdhan branches is only 78, or an average of 39 per branch.

As a result, staff utilization averages only 26%. For a branch to attain viability or increase its profits it is essential to ensure 100% staff utilization.

The income of a branch comes from its loan disbursement, based on a diversified and growing loan portfolio. Loan disbursement is very low in Nirdhan and a diversified portfolio has not been developed.

Internal fund management is one of the most important factors for the financial viability of an organization. But in case of Nirdhan, savings mobilization through the group fund is low and these funds are not used for on-lending but are deposited in the commercial bank. Cash control is also weak, leading to loss of potential earnings.

As a result of all these factors, Nirdhan's operating cost is high, its disbursement cost per unit is high, and because of their low investment their interest earning is quite low. On current performance it seems impossible for Nirdhan to achieve a viable branch.

However, we are confident that this situation can change. Nirdhan is operating in a very high potential area. The scope to form more groups and centres is very good. With more efficient branch management, an action plan for expansion, and proper training of staff, Nirdhan could make its branches viable.

Recommendations

1 The respective FA must be responsible for continuous group training of each new group. This training should be conducted for a minimum of seven days for one hour each day. This is very essential for all members to get a clear idea about the rules and regulations. This training should not be conducted by a facilitator. A lack of training and understanding of the main objectives and philosophy of the Nirdhan operation will eventually lead to poor credit discipline.

Like GB, Nirdhan can initiate a meeting with the husbands and adult children of members. This meeting can be held on the last day of continuous group training.

2 Nirdhan should introduce membership application forms like those used by GB. These forms should include all the personal and economic data of member's households, like the husband's or father's name, occupations, total cultivated land, house condition, number of children and level of education. They should note which month is the most critical period of the year and detail current assets and income. With the help of these forms, the impact of the project can easily be evaluated in the future.

3 The group is the first step of organizational structure in Nirdhan. A poor and landless woman becomes a project member through group formation. The group recognition test is the most vital gateway for maintaining quality control over the groups and centres. We feel that those who are directly involved with group selection and training cannot test the group. So, the group recognition test (GRT) should be conducted by the General Secretary. Otherwise the Branch Manager (BM) is likely to be too 'soft' and neither the Field Assistant nor the group members will take the GRT seriously.

4 Project Nirdhan is a non-political organization. It must always be neutral. At the time of the GRT they should not take any help from the member of the *panchayat* (representative of the local government).

5 The centre is known as the second step of the Grameen Bank organizational structure. The centre house is known as 'Bank for the Poor'. Discipline is the key to credit success. So centre discipline is very essential. We observed that because there is no proper place for the centre meeting it is very difficult to maintain discipline at the centre meeting. We feel that it is essential for every centre to have its own centre house with enough space for appropriate seating. Also every centre should have a 'sign board' stating the centre number and the centre name. This will help to motivate members and develop a centre identity.

  The seating arrangement of the group members in the centre meeting should be routinized. The group chairperson (GC) should sit on the far right, the group secretary should sit next left with the rest of the members sitting on the left of the group secretary. The first group should sit at the front of the centre meeting with other groups sitting behind them according to their group number. This makes it easier for the payments to pass along the row to the group chairperson, for attendance to be easily checked and the identity of the group to be emphasized.

6 Project Nirdhan should change the time of the centre meeting. Afternoon meetings make it impossible for the collection to be banked and make house-to-house visits and group training more difficult. With proper motivation members can be persuaded to change the centre meeting from evening to morning. All new centres should fix their meeting times in the morning.

7 100% attendance at the centre meeting is one of the preconditions of 100%

loan recovery. At the time of our visit attendance at centre meetings was 88% on average. Regular attendance should be emphasized. The member who fails to attend the meeting on time without sufficient reason should be penalized by the centre meeting. Otherwise absenteeism can become a chronic disease. To do this effectively the General Secretary will need to conduct surprise visits to centre meetings. If there is any negligence he will discuss the problem with the members.

8 The leadership responsibility of Centre Chief and Group Chairperson is very important to maintain overall discipline at the centre level. We observed a lack of Centre Chief and Group Chairperson responsibility in Nirdhan. They do not know their duties and responsibilities. We suggest that after selection of new Group Chairpersons the branch should arrange a workshop attended by the General Secretary, where their leadership role is discussed. The same should be done for newly-elected Centre Chiefs.

9 Contrary to GB procedures, the Branch Managers in Nirdhan approve loan proposals. There are some irregularities in the loan approval process. Project Nirdhan is a new organization and all the staff at branch level are newly appointed. So the Branch Manager should not be authorized to approve the loan proposal. Only the General Secretary should be authorized to approve loans. At the time of loan approval the General Secretary will check the purpose of the loan, the amount, the quality of the centre, full repayment of the previous loan, regular attendance at the weekly centre meeting, habit of repayment, recommendations of the Centre Chief, FA and Branch Manager. The General Secretary should also check that staggered disbursement using the 2:2:1 method is strictly followed.

Unlike GB procedure, Nirdhan loan disbursement is done at the centre meeting. This could create problems of security. We recommend that loans be disbursed at the Branch office.

10 The FA collects weekly instalments at the centre meeting without entering them into a collection sheet. This practice should be stopped immediately. A prescribed collection sheet should be used for every centre meeting and should be signed by both the FA and the Centre Chief.

11 Whether Group Tax One is refundable or not still it is a matter of confusion among the members and the FAs. Management should take a decision about Group Tax One and circulate it immediately.

12 Nirdhan charges a 10% 'administrative charge' on its loans. We feel they should increase the interest rate to a level comparable with the commercial bank lending rate. This interest should be charged using the reducing balance method.

13 Group fund is the savings fund of the group. It is not a savings fund of all members of the branch. Contrary to GB procedures the Branch office keeps a group fund account in a commercial bank. All the group fund savings of the branch are daily deposited in that account. Even savings of centre funds are also deposited in this group fund account. We suggest that each group fund account should be maintained group-wise and centre fund should be separate from group fund. The Branch office should open a group fund account for each group and then they can easily invest this fund amongst the borrowers at an interest rate of 10%, earning a profit margin of 4% (10%-6%).

[For Nirdhan to be able to do this legally, under Indian law, it would need to be transformed into a Non-Bank Financial Company under the Companies Act. — Editor's Note.]

14 All the project activities are implemented through the branch to the centre level. It is essential for the head office to know what is happening at the centre level. At present, except the General Secretary, they have no branch supervision officer. A specialized supervision officer should be appointed. His main duty will be to ensure the branch is following project rules and regulations in their day-to-day operations. In his supervision, he will check the overall discipline of the centres through surprise visits, financial control, loan utilization, problems and weaknesses of the centres and the activities of the field staff.

15 Nirdhan has no real staff training system. This is a fatal weakness because the Grameen approach requires rigorously trained, specialized field staff. A training programme should be prepared immediately. If possible they should arrange a minimum two months practical staff training in Bangladesh to observe the Grameen approach.

16 It seems that remuneration of staff is inadequate. It is hoped that staff salaries and benefits will be increased within the capacity of Nirdhan.

17 Nirdhan has no operational and accounting manual. This should be prepared as early as possible.

18 A monitoring system should be developed. The General Secretary should be exclusively responsible for monitoring branch activities. He can monitor branch activities in two ways: through collecting regular statistical data from the branch office and through branch and centre visits and through discussion with the members and staff.

The Branch Manager will be responsible for preparing regular and accurate monitoring reports using specific formats detailing the work progress of his branch. All the FAs will collect data for their respective centres and submit this information to the Branch Manager who will consolidate the information into a branch-wide report. For this purpose Nirdhan can introduce weekly and monthly statements, such as i) weekly loan evaluation statement ii) weekly attendance, instalment and savings statement iii) weekly fund management statement iv) monthly statistical statement.

19 Serious lack of control has been observed in respect of fund management. We observed huge amounts of cash being kept at the branch office for months at a time. This practice should be stopped. Idle funds have no productivity. The General Secretary must check the respective branches' weekly fund position. When he feels that the branch office is keeping a large amount of money without planning to disburse it he will be ask the respective Branch Manager to explain why he is keeping an unreasonable amount. If there is no adequate reason, the General Secretary must insist that the money be transfered to head office. For proper fund management day-to-day disbursement should be introduced.

20 The ratio of operating cost to income in Nirdhan is too high. Income must be increased. Income depends on investment and investment depends on groups. So Nirdhan has to increase the number of groups. Proper staff utilization is important to minimize the cost of staff services for each branch. Therefore the head office will try to ensure 100% utilization of staff in the project.

Multiple loans may be disbursed to members according to their needs, like small house loans, seasonal loans, tube-well loans, sanitary loans and others.

21 Nirdhan's disbursement cost per unit is increasing day by day. If the branch is to achieve financial viability then their disbursement cost per unit must must be less than Rs0.10. This is possible if the number and amount of loans is increased.

22 A project plan is a map of future goals and how the branches are to get there. Nirdhan has no plan and no projected budget for expenditure. A plan must be put in place so that the staff have objectives and quotas. Because the FAs are 100% responsible for implementing any plan, it must be worked out bottom to top, with their full involvement. The plan may be quarterly, half-yearly and annually. But the budget must be year-based.

The evaluation team feels that project Nirdhan is operating in areas that have a huge concentration of poor people providing excellent potential for establishing viable branches. In order to achieve this, there has to be a committed leadership at the Head Office backed up by a cadre of well-trained and committed field staff. The evaluation team believes that this is achievable with proper motivation, training and guidance.

Can Nirdhan Expand?

In the wake of this report, the Nirdhan General Secretary, Mr Sen Gupta, instituted an overhaul of the administrative and financial procedures of Nirdhan. A set of new forms were designed to control staff work, centre collection, cash control at the branch, group fund loans and other matters criticized by the Grameen Bank evaluators. Regular reporting from the branch to Head office and formats for branch visits and inspection by head office staff were also introduced.[7]

An internal audit was instituted, run by the accountant from SARS, who checked the branches on a weekly basis. In addition, external auditors were appointed to run quarterly checks on Nirdhan's accounts.

Nirdhan's long-suffering 'trainee assistants' found their salaries raised from an average of Rs640 (US$21) in 1994 to an average of close to Rs1,200 (US$39) per month by end 1995.[8] To strengthen the supervisory role of the head office and provide an officer who could conduct group recognition tests and centre visits, a programme officer was appointed to service the three branches and sent to a Grameen Trust/CASHPOR training workshop on credit discipline.

Head office staff and the SARS board worked out a detailed plan to scale up the pilot project into an institutionally viable programme. This plan visualizes filling up each branch to a maximum of 1,400 to 2,000 members over the next five years, and breaking even by the end of 1997. In the process, field staff salaries will rise to between Rs1,500 and Rs2,000 and five additional field staff will be employed. It is this master plan which will provide the framework for branch-level targets of group formation and disbursement to be set, so that staff performance can be better monitored.[9]

The question that confronts Nirdhan, however, is how to persuade donors to fund this expansion plan, given the extent and range of problems revealed by the Rashidull-Salam evaluation report. Although the evaluation reports of the other three replications were critical on specific issues, all got an overall positive endorsement from their evaluators. The evaluation team who reported on Nirdhan West Bengal recognized that the project had reached and benefited poor women, but they faulted its operations across-the-board for weaknesses in centre management, financial management, branch supervision and planning.

The other three replication projects, on the basis of their track record and the efforts of their chief executives, have all attracted funds to scale-up their pilot projects into expanding programmes. This includes support from outside agencies, like Grameen Trust, CIDSE, etc., and, for Nirdhan Nepal and SHARE, funds for on-lending from national commercial or development banks. Only Nirdhan West Bengal had not attracted additional funding for scaling-up some six months after the end of the pilot project.

In terms of actual performance, by end-November 1995, Nirdhan's three branches were reaching 853 members, well below the 2,100 reached by Nirdhan Nepal and Tau Yew Mai, and the 1,400 reached by SHARE at that time. Moreover, Nirdhan West Bengal's members are spread over three branches. With an average of 284 members per branch they are a very long way from viability. Nirdhan Nepal and SHARE already have one viable branch apiece, and realistic plans to bring their remaining branches up to self-sufficiency. It is this evidence of successful financial management that has persuaded local banks to extend them funds for on-lending.

Nirdhan West Bengal's unit costs are fairly low. Although its field assistants are on average reaching only 95 borrowers apiece, its unit cost of disbursing one rupee is 0.32 cents — a lower cost than SHARE. Because of its low costs, Nirdhan in mid-1995 was meeting half of its expenditure from its interest income of 16% on its loans.[10] However, this result was not based on the Grameen model of staff used to maximum efficiency to reach 300-400 borrowers per field assistant with a varied portfolio of financial services, all generating income. Rather it was simply based on very poorly-paid staff, serving less than 1,000 borrowers. There is also a large subsidy involved in the fact that the General Secretary of SARS is serving as project manager on a voluntary basis.

The lack of investment in staff development was the issue of greatest concern to CASHPOR and APDC during the pilot project and was not resolved, despite some increases in field staff salaries. CASHPOR argued that it was impossible to build a basis for expansion on such poorly-paid, temporary staff and voluntarist head office management. The whole purpose of Phase Three of APDC's replication programme was to lay the basis to institutionalize pilot projects into full-scale credit and savings programmes able to impact on large numbers of poor women. Nirdhan West Bengal's failure to use the pilot period (during which it had adequate funding) to lay a foundation for expansion, meant that by 1995 it was in a precarious financial position, with minimal funds in reserve[11] and no immediate prospect of support from donors or banks.[12] Without interim funding, it seemed unlikely that they would be able to upgrade staff salaries and efficiency, or expand to any substantial number of borrowers.

Notes

1. Ray, 1987. *To Chase a Miracle: A Study of the Grameen Bank in Bangladesh*, University Press Ltd., Dhaka.
2. Project Proposal to APDC.
3. Ray to Gibbons, CASHPOR, 27 July 1994.
4. Ray to Dr Somsak, APDC, October 3 1994.
5. This and subsequent quotes from Mr Wijewardena are all from the Mid-Term Evaluation Report, to APDC.
6. Dr Somsak, APDC to Ray, 21 July 1994.

7. Personal communication from Mr Sen Gupta to Gibbons, February 1996.

8. Ray, *Final Report on Project Nirdhan in West Bengal,* February 1996.

9. Expansion Plan sent to CASHPOR, June 1996.

10. Calculated from Ray, *Final Report.*

11. Audited Financial Statement, 1 April 1994 to 31 March 1995.

12. In September, 1996, Nirdhan West Bengal succeeded in getting scaling-up funds, as a soft loan, from Grameen Trust, in order to bring its Hasnabad branch to viability. Letter from Sen Gupta to CASHPOR.

4

Tau Yew Mai, Vietnam

DAVID S. GIBBONS AND HELEN TODD

THE TAU YEW MAI PROJECT of the Women's Union of Vietnam is the first attempt to replicate the Grameen Bank model in a Communist state. Whether it can succeed in this attempt is of great importance in Vietnam, where millions still live in poverty. Its adaptation to a monolithic government structure and a liberalizing economy also hold important lessons for China, which has the second largest population of poor in the world, next to India. The process of implementing the Grameen Bank model in Vietnam laid bare some of the assumptions which underlie both the model and the organization which did the transplanting.

The Grameen Bank model presupposes, at least implicitly, an exploitative landlord-moneylender class which dominates opportunity and the political structure in the rural village. It is this élite that has captured the subsidized credit directed to the rural areas by governments in the name of poverty reduction. The Grameen Bank model deals with this by politely sidestepping the local power structure and working directly with a targeted group of landless, poor women. The discipline of weekly meetings, weekly repayments and a very public fraternizing with the village underclass discourage non-poor women from participating. GB is non-governmental, and is therefore not obliged to work through political brokers and government agencies, which either comprise, or work hand-in-glove with, the local élite. Its staff are full-time professionals posted outside their home areas in order to avoid kin and clan pressures.

In Vietnam, land reform eliminated the landlord class. Theoretically all land is owned by the state and families are alloted usufruct rights by the commune-level farmers' association on the basis of their labour power. The élite in the commune is a political one, which, in theory at least, is not an exploitative class but represents the people. The idea of using an NGO to sidestep the government structure and reach the poor directly is entirely foreign in Vietnam. Until very recently NGOs did not exist. Everything that reaches the rural people is mediated through the people's committees and their closely-related mass organizations.

Inequalities exist, of course, and they are growing with economic liberalization. We found moneylending, at brutal rates, very common in the villages. Poverty is widespread; but there are no 'landless' as in Bangladesh or India or the Philippines. The credit programme as it was implemented by the Women's Union was seen simply as a method that the existing political structure could adopt to reduce rural poverty — and which would boost their popularity in the process. An early project status report listed as the third important achievement: 'Women's Union work is more attractive and practical to women [in the commune]. The role of the Vietnam Women's Union is improved and enhanced.'[1]

The Women's Union, which was founded in 1930, is *the* mass organization for mobilizing women throughout Vietnam. It works in tandem with the Communist Party at all levels, from the commune, to district, provincial and national levels. With a membership of 11 million women it now plays a powerful role in development, particularly in the social welfare areas of health, family planning and mother and child care. More recently it has felt the need to strengthen women's economic base through various livelihood programmes, including credit. All of the Women's Union programmes are implemented at commune level through the cadres who make up the Women's Union executive committee. These are women of the village, who farm and trade like other rural families. As elected leaders, however, they work closely with the people's committee, they wield considerable local power and they are paid allowances for their work.

For the leaders of the Women's Union, who have devoted their lives to this development work, it is inconceivable that the political structure in the commune, of which they are such an integral part, should be regarded as 'exploitative' or excluded from the administration of the credit programme. So it was inevitable that when the credit programme was introduced, it should be administered by the women's union cadres who already ran the health and family planning programmes in the commune.

At head office level in Hanoi, the Women's Union is a large and powerful organization, and has attracted well-qualified and capable women into its staff. Project Director, Mdm Do Thi Tan and Project Manager, Mdm Lee Thi Lan are highly motivated women who have each worked in the Union for more than 20 years.

Initially, the Tau Yew Mai project was very much a child of the replication movement. In 1992, CIDSE, an international group of Catholic development agencies working in Vietnam since 1988, hired a Filipino, J. Aristotle (Aries) Alip, as its credit adviser. He is the Founding President of CARD in the Philippines, which began a replication of the Grameen Bank model there in 1990. It was Mr Aries who convinced the Women's Union Central Committee to consider a Grameen-type credit programme in early 1992 and they appointed him their adviser. Mr Aries arranged for the training of five Women's Union staff at the GB replications of CARD and Project Dungganon in the Philippines for two months, followed by a month at the Grameen Bank. When the project began, two senior staffers from CARD helped to train the field staff in two communes, and conducted a refresher workshop for management staff in Hanoi.

Mr Aries Alip christened the new programme *Tau Yew Mai*, a racy southern way of saying 'I love you.' This phrase is so colloquial that the proper ladies of the Women's Union translate it as 'The Affection Fund.'

Tau Yew Mai (TYM) began operations in the Minh Phu commune of Soc San District, disbursing its first loans in August, 1992. Minh Phu is a windswept, flat and infertile plain some 50km north of Hanoi, where poverty is severe, with an average monthly income of around US$15 per household. The structure was textbook Grameen, with the formation of groups and centres, small loans, weekly repayment and compulsory savings. But the initial reliance on part-time cadre field staff, rooted in their localities and influential members of it, made Tau Yew Mai, in fact, a much more *managed,* top-down programme than Grameen Bank or the other three replications featured in this book. The dominance of local cadres over the centres — and the difficulty of supervising them from head office — led to a number of problems which will be described later in this chapter.

In the nature of its economy, however, — and in the nature of its women — Tau Yew Mai was much *better* placed than the other three replications to take advantage of the provision of credit Grameen style. Rural women in Vietnam are full economic actors; they are seen everywhere in the fields and the markets. There are no cultural or religious constraints on their economic activities and women comprise 71% of the petty traders in Vietnam. Most women are literate and can keep accounts. Both tradition and the absence of men at war have given them the key to the family cashbox. Because of the Communist revolution, most commune families have the basic resource of land — a large houselot for raising animals and usufruct over at least one-third of an acre of cropping land. Putting credit into the hands of these active and resourceful women is a bit like adding yeast to dough. Their incomes have taken off and are being rapidly converted into assets.

The Tau Yew Mai project has benefited from a flood of aid funds into Hanoi. After being blacklisted by nearly every donor in the world for 20 years, Vietnam is suddenly the darling of the aid industry. The outreach and professionalism of the Women's Union have made it an attractive partner for many of these agencies.

Major project funding was provided by the Asian Community Trust of Japan, with additional funds coming from APDC, Nissan Foundation and RKK of Japan, the Grameen Trust and Canada World Relief. In 1995, in its third year of operation, TYM received pledges of funding for two new branches from Catholic Relief Services, from Oxfam America and substantial funds from CIDSE. It is the only one of the four replications which has not had funding worries dogging its expansion.

The downside of the Women's Union's popularity with donors is that it has not been forced, like SHARE and Nirdhan Nepal, to find local sources for on-lending funds — and to pay the interest rates levied by local bank lenders. This process may be painful, but it makes the programme independent of donors and, at full operation, sustainable for as long as it is needed by its borrowers.

Professor Yunus of Grameen Bank has been very supportive of the Vietnam replication. On his visit to the project in December 1994 he lobbied senior government figures to allow the transformation of TYM into a women's bank, under its own charter, with professionally qualified and adequately paid staff. 'A country that can produce Ho Chi Minh and win a war against America, can surely eliminate poverty,' he commented.[2]

CASHPOR has also taken a particular interest in this project, excited by the prospect of getting a GB replication to work in a country with such a high level of poverty — and in the implications for China of adapting the model to a socialist context. CASHPOR monitoring has been followed through with considerable inputs in training and technical assistance whenever the need appeared. Its main frustration has been getting the *forms* of Grameen Banking adopted, while seeing their actual content lost whenever it hit up against local practice.

For example, in July 1994 CASHPOR helped TYM organize a workshop in Hanoi on targeting poor women. CASHPOR's training manual on targeting was translated into Vietnamese and Prof. Sukor Kassim, former Deputy MD of AIM, worked with TYM staff to develop a housing index relevant to north Vietnam and a systematic way of mapping potential branch and centre areas. Later Gibbons and Todd observed the poverty mapping done in a non-poor commune because the Women's Union there demanded it and the housing index stretched to include the Women's Union leader in that commune.

TYM has had policy support from all levels of government, where there is a real concern, not only about poverty, but about the increasing polarization which has followed the opening of the Vietnamese economy to the world. TYM's operation in the Vietnam context, however, has brought a number of bureaucratic hassles, particularly in financial management. It took two years, for example to set up a branch office in the project area and this office found it very difficult to get permission even to open a separate bank account. For months staff were forced to keep large amounts of cash in a cupboard. External auditing of government agency accounts is not a normal practice in Vietnam, and it is not done for TYM, despite the hackles this raises with donors.

Government salaries in Vietnam are extremely low, and employees only make ends meet through the housing, rice and other subsidies available to government officials. Structuring a staff salary scheme for an 'independent' project within this system is fraught with conflicts. In addition, job opportunities are rarely advertised in Vietnam, so recruitment of project staff invariably means hiring relatives (albeit well-qualified) of Womens' Union officials.[3]

The Pilot Years

'Credit is a new activity for the Women's Union, but the demand amongst the women is so strong that sometimes I feel as if I am sitting on a runaway horse,' commented Project Director, Mdm Do Thi Tan, a year after the project began.[4] At Minh Phu, where the first groups were formed in August 1992, there are 1,800 households. No less than 600 women registered to join the programme after it was announced, of whom only 11 were selected to join the first training programme. Four cadres were chosen as field assistants (FAs), including the President of the Minh Phu Women's Union Committee, and given allowances for running the centre meetings and training groups. In a few months, TYM started operations in two nearby communes and soon had a total of 13 FAs, all local cadres of the Women's Union.

In its first 18 months of operation, TYM reached 702 members and disbursed US$24,550 in loans. Only around 30% of those who had registered to join in the three communes had been able to get in, and demand was still strong. The FAs were forming between one and 1.5 groups each per month. The management team and the Women's Union Central Committee were very enthusiastic about the project's success. When Professor David Gibbons visited for the mid-term assessment for APDC, they told him that TYM was the most hopeful programme run by the Women's Union. Gibbons was equally enthusiastic. He was delighted by the response and the impact in the field and he concluded that a good basis was being laid for expansion towards financial viability.

The areas of concern in the process of expansion, he pointed out, were the institutional shape of TYM and its staffing and the setting of an interest rate that would cover costs and inflation. He noted that total interest income on funds disbursed to date was only 4.8% per annum, while inflation was running at around 7%. He recommended that interest rates should be at least 20% per annum to attain viability.

TYM's costs were lower than any replication Gibbons had seen. Because the field work was done by part-time staff and the management team salaries were paid by the Women's Union, salary costs were only 8.7% of operating expenditure. In other GB replications staff costs amounted to around 70% of expenditure. The staff had been very successful so far — centre discipline was good and defaults were zero. But Gibbons questioned whether part-time staff could run the project at a much larger scale of operation. He warned that as TYM institutionalized, its staff would probably have to be appointed to full-time positions and paid adequate salaries.

Growth — and Enthusiasm — Level Off

In October 1994, after two years of managing the project field staff long-distance from Hanoi, TYM set up a branch office at the district town of Soc San. A branch manager, who is the vice-president of the Women's Union at district level, and an accountant, set up shop and tried to extend Grameen-style financial supervision over the 13 cadres — which promptly brought some of the underlying problems of the project out into the open.

The cadres, who were accustomed to keeping the loan ledgers in their houses, and updating them when they saw fit, were now required to report three times a week to the branch office and keep the records under the eye of the branch manager. The president of the women's union committee in Minh Phu, one of the field assistants, threatened to resign if she was forced to cycle to Soc San three days a week. When the project insisted, she did resign — and took more than 100 members out of TYM with her.

Suddenly it became clear that the members owed their loyalty not to their groups and centres but to the local official who had selected and trained them, and that her hold over them was stronger than their need for credit.

The other FAs complied with the new system of record keeping, but most resisted field supervision. The branch manager took the line of least resistance and concentrated on the accounts, seldom visiting the centres.

Since the FAs could rely on their official authority to compel repayment, some of them bypassed the centres and got the centre chief to collect the repayments and deliver them to the FAs house. Most decisions were taken by the FAs, so the centres ceased to have much function, and attendance at the weekly meetings dropped. Cadres were in a position to be partial in their selection of members and, in fact, a number of non-poor got into the programme. Without close field supervision, they were able to abuse their office in other ways. Some months after the branch office opened, it was discovered that a field assistant had connived at a group of women joining two centres at once and getting double loans. Some of their repayments never reached the branch office, so she had taken her reward for bending the rules by pocketing some of their payments. This episode showed the failure of the group recognition test (GRT), since house visits would have uncovered this fraud before any loans were disbursed. This FA had to be dismissed, after much recrimination in the commune, and more members left the programme.

Problems with the field staff had a knock-on effect on new group formation and loan disbursement. Both had been rising steadily through 1993 and the first quarter of 1994, when membership passed the 1,000 mark. In the second half of 1994 membership growth levelled off and in the first quarter of 1995 it dropped. Membership did not start growing strongly again until the second half of 1995.

The TYM management team were shaken by what they saw as a betrayal of trust in the 'double membership' case and there was some questioning in the Women's Union Central Committee about the value of targeting credit on only poor women. These doubts came at a time when CIDSE and other donors were pressing to offer funding to expand into new branches.

As a result, a policy decision was taken to go ahead with one new branch and recruit full-time staff to run it. Four full-time trainees, all college graduates, were recruited and attatched to the Soc San branch office for training. Subsequently,

Figure 4.1: TYM Membership Growth: July1993-Dec.1995

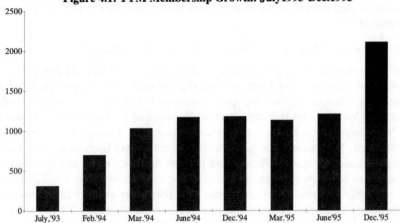

another seven trainees, both university and college graduates, were recruited to staff the new branch. There were still doubts, however, about whether young graduates would have the 'prestige' to form groups and run centres like the older, locally-based Women's Union cadres.

It was in this state of flux and debate within the Women's Union about how they should go ahead that Professor Gibbons and Helen Todd visited TYM in May 1995. They found the management team in a sombre mood. From being the most hopeful programme of the Women's Union, it had become the one producing the most headaches. After a week in the field, Gibbons' report was very critical of the top-down cadre management of the centres and he put his weight, and the technical support of CASHPOR, behind the change to full-time professional management that was already beginning to take place.

Gibbons' final evaluation report, which analyses the weaknesses in the Soc San branch and recommends the changes which would facilitate expansion to new branches, is reproduced in abridged form in the following section.

Weaknesses in Soc San 1

There are a number of indications that TYM is running a kind of 'administered Grameen Banking', which will tend to undermine the development of collective responsibility among the borrowers. Genuine Grameen Banking builds the resilience of its groups and centres through the self-selection of members and their participation in the centre meeting processes of loan approval, repayment and checking of loan use. Deviations from this participatory model were observed, although it is not known how widespread they are. They are detailed here because of their potential for undermining the success that TYM has achieved so far.

There are other weaknesses in supervision, field-staff training and branch planning which need to be addressed by TYM management. Solutions should be found so that the errors made in the first branch are not repeated in the newer branches.

Pre-selection of eligible borrowers by commune officials

In some communes prior to group formation, the president of the Women's Union at the commune level, in consultation with other commune officials, draws up a list of the 'reliable' poor households. These women are then called by the TYM staff for training. After explanation of the objectives and rules of TYM, they were asked to form groups of five from among those present and interested. This means that potential borrowers do not form their own groups themselves from among like-minded persons that they know and trust. Rather they have to form their groups from among those selected by the TYM staff. This is likely to result in weak groups with few if any strong bonds among the members. Subsequently group members are likely to blame the TYM staff if any member becomes a problem for the group. Collective responsibility will not develop easily and peer group support and pressure may not be forthcoming.

Too Poor for TYM?

Some FAs, Women's Union and local officials at commune level have expressed the opinion to us that the poorest of the poor are 'too poor' to join TYM. So long as members are pre-selected by these officials, the poorest will be effectively excluded from the programme. Unfortunately, female-headed households are often included in this group. These women, on their own with young children, are already disadvantaged in the allocation of land by the commune committee, because they lack labour power.

In Bac Phu we interviewed two women whom the Women's Union had already decided would not be allowed to become members, because they had been abandoned by their husbands and had young children. Both said initially: 'How could I repay?' When it was pointed out that the weekly repayment was 4,000 Dong + 1,000 savings, they said they could manage that by selling their labour for one day. They were not sure if they could persuade four neighbours to join them to form a group, but they would try.

So long as the decision is in the hands of the local authorities, and so long as *they* take the responsibility for forming groups and getting the repayment, they will not take the risk of allowing the very poor, particularly women on their own, into TYM. In other projects, including GB, widows and divorcees are often the best borrowers — because they are the most desperate.

In fact these important elements of the GB model do not appear to be considered important by the staff. It is the FAs who are taking primary responsibility for savings mobilization, loan approval and repayment. Groups and centres are not being given important roles in these matters, except for those centre chiefs who are required, against the rules, to bring repayments to the homes of the field staff. TYM is being administered by its field staff, all of whom are members of the Executive Committee of the Women's Union at the commune level. It is not in any meaningful way a participatory programme.

Misunderstanding and misuse of group fund

The basic purposes of the Group Fund (savings mobilization, giving strength to the Group, security and on-lending funds for the project) are not being met by the way it is administered. Two-thirds of the balance in the group funds have been available for borrowing, and members have come to use it as a source of supplementary loans, especially for agriculture. Balances in the group funds are small, thus providing little loan security and on-lending funds for TYM, and nothing is left for member emergencies. Moreover Group Tax 1 and Group Tax 2 are withdrawn along with personal savings when a member leaves a group, thus further depleting its group fund. Groups are not being strengthened by their group funds, as is intended under the GB model. Almost all the money is out in the hands of borrowers as supplementary loans, so no money is available for peer group support and collective responsibility.

Group and centre officials not rotated

Most group chairpersons and centre chiefs have continued in office once being selected. Their term is not restricted to one year, as required under the GB model. According to TYM staff, the members do not want to change their officials. As a result there is no training in, nor experience of, leadership for most of the women. There is a danger of groups and centres becoming 'captured' by the more clever, articulate and aggressive women and subsequently manipulated primarily for their own benefit in collusion with the local party officials.

Minimal supervision of fieldstaff

The field staff of TYM are all village-level cadres of the Women's Union. They work part-time; they are mainly middle-aged women with considerable experience and clout in the commune. Perhaps for these reasons, the Branch Manager appears to have little supervisory control over them. The Branch Manager is not field-oriented. Her primary responsibility appears to be the control of cash at the branch office. Under the GB model, a branch manager is responsible for the overall operation of the branch, and primarily concerned with supervision of the field staff. This is done through scheduled and unscheduled field and centre visits. In TYM the main mechanism for communication between the staff and the branch is the weekly meeting at the branch office. But since most of the financial transactions take place at the weekly centre meetings, in the village, it is essential for a branch manager to know what is going on at the centres through periodic centre visits, including surprise visits.

Similarly, branch managers and field staff should be supervised by more senior staff. Under the GB model this is done by Area Managers and Programme Officers, who are also primarily field-oriented. They supervise through scheduled and unscheduled centre and branch visits, as well as through the monthly meeting of branch managers.

Very little field supervision of the kind required under Grameen Banking is taking place in TYM. Probably this is because the local-level officals of the Women's Union are administering the programme at the commune level, and the WU officials at the District and Hanoi levels expect them to do the work properly. In addition, the higher-level officials appear to feel that surprise visits by them to centres and branches would be seen as evidence of distrust of the field staff. This is one indication of a lack of business-like thinking and practices in the project. The most important quality control procedure under the GB model, the Group Recognition Test (GRT), is not being carried out independently of the branch staff as is required. As TYM does not yet have an Area Manager nor a Programme Officer, the GRT should be carried out by a member of the project management and it must include a visit to each potential member's house (not being done currently by TYM). Otherwise the project has no independent check on the quality of the targeting, nor of group formation and group training.

Lack of centre discipline and a suitable meeting place

There are indications that some scheduled centre meetings have not been held, that the fieldstaff responsible have not attended some of their centre meetings and that attendance by members is not always satisfactory. Meetings are held in members' houses and usually there is not enough space for members of the larger centres to sit. Some have to sit in separate rooms and even outside. As a result it is difficult to conduct the meeting in a business-like manner. No independent check is carried out by the project management team on centre discipline.

Weak financial control between centre and branch

There is a 'gaping hole' in the financial control between centre and branch, because the groups do not receive any offical receipt showing that their payments have reached the branch. This can be done simply by the cashier stamping 'received' on the blue carbon copy of the group collection sheet and signing her name. Then the blue copy should be returned by the FA to the group chairperson at the following centre meeting. Members should be trained to compare it with their (red) copy of the collection sheet that was retained by the group the previous week. Any alterations must have been signed by the branch manager. The FA should be given the receipt for the total collection of the centre, that is prepared by the cashier, for her own records.

Staff in Transition

The scene is a weekly staff meeting of Soc San 1, the first branch. Thirteen part-time FAs are attending, tough looking, middle-aged women in black peasant trousers, who exude authority. The acting branch manager, an attractive young graduate in tailored slacks and blouse, conducts the meeting. She is a bit diffident and the FAs tend to switch off when she speaks. Seven graduate trainees sit at one side. The project team of Mdm Tan, Mdm Lan and Mdm Van have come from Hanoi. Everybody listens to *them*.

The FA from Phu Minh has a problem. One of her members took a second loan of Dong 700,000, paid for eight weeks, and then disappeared from her house and the commune. They are pressuring her husband to repay, but he says: 'She took the loan. She took all the money with her. Why should I pay?'

An increasingly hot discussion follows, in which most of the FAs line up on the side of coercion and the Branch Manager argues, Grameen-style, for understanding the woman's situation and getting the group to take responsibility for her. The project team let it rage, then, diplomatically, they come down on the side of the branch manager.

'Ask the centre members and also the Women's Union to talk to the family and find out what is wrong and try to get the group to take responsibility for repayment in the meantime,' suggests the BM.

'How can I ask the group to pay?', asks the FA. 'She is not in difficulties. She left deliberately!'

'We shouldn't ask the members. We should report her to the people's committee. The husband has a good radio. They can make him sell it to repay the loan. A husband must take responsibility for his wife!' stated another FA.

'The group and centre made a bad decision giving a large loan to a member without knowing her well. So they have to take responsibility now she has absconded,' countered the BM.

'There is some blame to the centre, but this member didn't do her duty and her husband is refusing to co-operate, so we should take them to the law,' said another FA.

Project Manager, Mdm Lan begins to question the FAs about the woman and gradually it emerges that she is 'an honest and ordinary person.' There is 'no conflict with her husband or in-laws'. 'She repaid faithfully before.' She has been missing for only one week. She is pregnant. She has no children. She has had three late miscarriages and one stillbirth.

There is a bit of a silence and the FA starts clicking away on her calculator to see if there is enough in the woman's group fund to cover her arrears.

'Convene a centre meeting with the husband and find out the reasons behind this. Be more patient,' Mdm Lan advises, 'she may come back. Try to help her and solve it within the centre.'

'Last time we went to the people's committee and asked them to take action against one of our members, they replied that we call ourselves the "Affection Fund" and how can we be so harsh!' commented Mdm Van, breaking the tension.

Later in the meeting, the FA who wanted to go to the law said that for larger loans they should also get the signature of the husband 'so if something happens we can force him to repay.'

Mdm Tan, Project Director, replies with some passion: 'The objective of this project is to boost the confidence and the abilities of women. There is no need to involve the husband in the process of loan approval. That is the business of the centre.'

Building the Future: Training and Planning

Systematic, practical training of field staff and branch managers is a dilemma for TYM, particularly with the opening of the second branch, Soc San 2. Those experienced FAs who are doing effective work cannot be transferred to the new branch as they are part-time and locally based. The new trainees recruited to staff the second branch are being given theoretical training through lectures from members of the project team who have themselves been trained at GB and CARD. But they are reluctant to assign new trainees to follow the existing part-time field staff in their work, in case they should learn bad habits. As a result the new staff are getting no practical training in group formation, group training, conduct of centre meetings and loan utilization checks.

The four trainees first recruited took over the centres formed by the two FAs who resigned. But most of these centres soon collapsed and the trainees returned to the branch where their experience was limited to accounts. They later joined the new batch of trainees doing poverty mapping for the new branch.

In mid-1995, the branch manager of Soc San I went to Bangladesh to do two months area manager training with the Grameen Bank, where she was fully exposed to the skills of field supervision. However, no branch manager has yet been selected for the second branch and one will probably be chosen from the best of the trainees.

Full-time staff

Grameen Banking requires full-time field and management staff. Except for the trainees, TYM's field and management staff are still part-time. As a result, eleven (formerly 13) field staff are being used to serve 1,140 members (an average of only 103 members per field staff). This imposes an impossible supervisory burden on the Branch Manager. Her span of control at 11 field-staff, one cashier and one bookkeeper is much too high to allow adequate supervision. The normal span of control for a branch manager under GB is eight. It has not been possible for the project management to get adequate and timely monitoring information from the part-time fieldstaff who say they are too busy to fill in the forms.

The decision to use full-time field staff in the new branches is very welcome, and 11 full-time trainees have been hired for this purpose. However, under the GB model new branches are opened in the poorest areas not yet served and by the branch manager designate. Usually he spends a couple of months doing a preliminary survey and forms the first groups. He becomes thoroughly familiar with the area and problems of group formation and can properly supervise his fieldstaff in these matters. TYM is trying to open a new branch without any trained branch manager designate and by sending newly-recruited trainees to do the area survey. Communes that are not among the poorest are being visited, and invalid information is being recorded. This is a dangerous way to start in a new area.

Major Impact on Income

Most borrowers seem to have made substantial gains in income after joining TYM. TYM's internal impact study in Minh Phu commune, where they have been working the longest, shows an average increase in income from a base of 26,654 Dong (US$2.66) per capita per month, to 44,290 Dong (US$4.42) by the end of the second year. The average increase in income in the first year of borrowing is 35%, increasing to 66% in the second year. This increase in income comes from the quite faithful investment of the general loan in projects, mainly livestock, and through the use of frequent group fund loans for agricultural inputs to improve the yield of paddy and vegetable fields.

Borrowers who invest in chicken, pig or duck raising (the majority of loans) are able to get a return within three to five months. Because of weekly repayment, all the proceeds from the sale of livestock are available for reinvestment, which enables a rapid build-up of assets. Many of these borrowers could successfully use more capital. Particularly, they could use a seasonal loan for cultivation inputs. Currently, the group fund loans of 100,000 Dong are in fact used as 'fertilizer loans'; but they are not large enough for this purpose (farmers say they need 50,000 to 100,000 Dong per *sau* per season) or between half and one million Dong per acre. Moreover, this use defeats the purpose of the group fund, which is for crisis consumption, in order to save families from resorting to moneylenders in emergencies.

The TYM Impact Study shows a total increase in assets of 78.2 million Dong (US$7,280) amongst their 542 member sample bought in the first two years of membership. These purchases included all repairs and new building in the houselot, furniture and appliances, new production equipment and cows and buffaloes. If the value of all assets in livestock, including pigs and poultry, had been included in this survey, the increase would have been considerably higher.

However, there *is* a group of borrowers where the increase in income is small and the impact on assets is likely to be slow, for the following reasons:

*   **Heavy burden of old debts at high interest rates.** Almost all the borrowers interviewed were indebted before they joined TYM. Most succeeded in paying off their debts from their profits within two years. Others were still paying, leaving little for reinvestment. A rice loan in the first year of borrowing, such as TYM implemented in Minh Phu, would help these families avoid borrowing paddy during times of hunger which must be repaid double at harvest time. TYM should be aware of this burden their members still carry and motivate them to clear old debts from their profits, not from their capital.

*   **Death/illness of animals.** Of the seven case studies collected, three women had lost their investment because their animals had died or had to be sold at

a loss because of illness. One women invested two loans in pigs and all died. Since the impact on her income was negative she has dropped out of TYM. The veterinary training TYM has given is one means of lessening the risk, but it should also consider an 'animal security fund' as practised by Nirdhan Nepal. In this scheme, 1% of any loan for livestock is deducted for insurance. If an animal dies, half the value of the loan is paid to the borrower so that she can restart her project.

- **Illness in the family.** Some borrowers have sold their livestock to treat illness, because the group fund has not been available for this kind of emergency. Proper use of the group fund would help prevent sale of productive assets for emergency consumption.

A second impact study carried out by TYM in Minh Phu commune at the end of 1995 shows even more positive impact on poor households.

After three years of borrowing, household monthly income per capita had doubled in the Phu Son hamlet and multiplied 2.8 times in Lien Phu. Its impact was strong among the poorest as well. The Ban Tien hamlet is the poorest in the Minh Phu commune, due to the poor quality of soil and isolation from transportation. Some 15 households out of the total 24 fell under TYM criteria and joined the project. Ten of them had three years membership in TYM. Hardly any of them had been absent from a centre meeting for the whole three years. They used to earn on average 22,560 Dong per month before the project. Their income has doubled to an average of 42,000 Dong in these three years. Eight of the ten built new houses; eight purchased cows and seven purchased bicycles. They always borrow the highest loan size available for every cycle — all have borrowed 1 million Dong (about US$91) for the third cycle. Their repayment over the three years has been faultless.

Project Manager, Mdm Lee Thi Lan, writes in the context of this second impact study:

> With very small weekly savings of 1,000 Dong each and 5% of the loan, 335 members (in Minh Phu) could save 8,252,929 Dong after 6 months. This is an achievement of great significance, not only economic but also psychological. The women cannot believe how big their group funds become after several years from such small weekly savings. These savings are used to make loans to the members from the second year if they encounter any difficulties. It is worth noting that no organization has made this kind of savings and loans possible for the poor before.
>
> When interviewed and asked to comment on the current operations of the project, all the members in the Soc San branch gave a common answer: the current mechanism is quite suitable for the poor. Moreover, it helps to make the atmosphere in their families more cheerful. This is demonstrated when the women had to attend the five days training course, they found that they got help from husbands, children, brothers and sisters so they had time to study at home. It was very important, especially for the illiterate members. Besides, the mechanism

Rapidly Rolling Credit

Three years ago Mdm Duong lived in a battered house into which water flooded every wet season. Abandoned by her husband years earlier, and left with two children, she was desperately poor. When she wanted to join the first TYM centre, other members had to be 'persuaded' to accept her because they feared she was too poor to repay weekly.

She borrowed only 200,000 Dong (US$20) to start. In the first year she rolled that capital three times and by the end of it had a million Dong in her hand. Her story illustrates how fast these women can move once they get access to even small amounts of capital.

She invested her 200,000 Dong in chickens, sold them three months later and reinvested in two piglets. They fattened well and after six months she sold them for 600,000 and reinvested in a backyard operation making clay bricks. Her son, now in his early 20s, helped and they made one million Dong from the first firing. Since the loan was repaid weekly through selling their labour, these lump sums remained intact as capital for reinvestment.

There was no second firing. Mdm Duong was planning ahead. She squirreled away the one million and sent her son to work with a housebuilder so that he could learn how it was done. Meanwhile she took her second loan of 500,000 Dong and bought two more piglets, built a pigsty and stocked up on pig feed.

Mdm Duong and her son and teenage daughter cultivate 7 *sau* (7/10ths of an acre) of land; only 3 *sau* are wet paddy; the rest is dry land. During these first two years she took three Group Fund loans which enabled her to cultivate vegetables with better returns — first peanuts, then cucumbers and tomatoes. She also bought fertilizer with her Group Fund to boost the paddy harvest.

In the second year she made her big move. She sold her boggy house and houselot; she sold her fat pigs for one million; she took out her savings. Altogether she rounded up nearly 5 million Dong. Then she bought a new houselot of 2.5 *sau* on high ground, bought all the materials for a new tiled house and called her son home to build it.

He came back with more than carpentry skills, however. He had built a house for a *tofu* maker and had learned the skill. So when Mdm Duong was eligible for her third loan of one million Dong she bought the equipment to make *tofu* and invested the rest in a pregnant sow and two piglets.

By May of her third year of borrowing she was running three nicely integrated businesses. Some of the pigs she sold and invested into a profitable crop — tobacco. The *tofu* business is producing a rich soy bean waste to feed her pigs. The pig manure is going on to her fields and the sale of tobacco is providing the working capital for the *tofu* business. Two days profit from the *tofu* business covers her repayment; the rest is pure jam. She is looking forward to her fourth loan so that she can wire her house and buy an electric soybean grinder.

'I cannot imagine what I would be without TYM. You can fatten a piglet and sell it, but without *more* capital each year then you cannot invest in cultivation, you cannot do much at all. All the women in my group are doing well and none of us are borrowing from moneylenders the way we had to do before. When we are short we help each other.'

of weekly meetings and instalments also brought a change in the member families. A lot of members told us that their husbands and children work much harder in order to raise enough money to pay the weekly instalments and give her time to attend the weekly meetings. Therefore, they not only fulfil the weekly instalments but also have some positive balance for covering their daily needs. The members said that everything that happens at the weekly meetings is related at home 'for entertaining and shortening the boring rural evenings'.

Women in Charge

Poor rural women in Vietnam are already employed in cultivation, processing and trading. However, if poor women in Bac Phu (where TYM plans to open a second branch) and three-year borrowers in Minh Phu are compared, Bac Phu women commonly sell their labour, while this seems to be rare amongst members in Minh Phu. This signals that one outcome of TYM membership is that women are liberated from daily labour and are working for themselves. Women who were asked about the extra work burden since joining TYM protested that they were organizing family members to help with their projects and that the extra income made any additional work burden more than worthwhile.

Women in Vietnam are not only active economically, including in petty trading, they also traditionally 'hold the key to the family cashbox'. It seemed that all the women borrowers were using their loans themselves and played a major role in deciding how to invest the profits. This should ensure that the increased income from TYM loans is used directly to improve the family food, clothing and house condition and for investment in their children's education and health. Many TYM members interviewed had already or were planning to improve the house structure, build kitchens, toilets and pigsties, plant fruit trees and build walls. Several said that they were using the extra income to keep younger children in school longer than their elder siblings.

As Mdm Mai from Minh Phu commented: 'We are doing the calculating for the family. If you put the money in the man's hand he might squander it, but if you put it in mine I will spend it for the family.'

Mdm Duong from Minh Phu, (see box on page 91) who lives with her married son, is very much in control of her household. 'It was my decision to start this business and I manage it. I sell the *tofu* and I keep the money. If my son wants something, if I think it is necessary, then I give him money.'

Overall, the impact of TYM loans on the borrowers is positive and strong, testimony that poor women in the hamlets have the skills and determination to use their loans effectively and have enough influence in the family to reinvest their profits for the benefit of the household. This is the fundamental strength of TYM.

Good Prospects for Financial Viability

In general Tau Yew Mai appears to have good prospects for attaining financial viability. Basically this is because its costs are low. The only doubt is that its interest rate – of 1.8% per month on a declining balance – is probably not enough.

Currently it is not possible to know if the existing Soc San Branch is on track for viability. Essentially this is because there is no separate accounting at the branch level as yet. Plans have been made to treat the branches as accounting units. As soon as this has been implemented in Soc San, its progress should be evaluated.

TYM has a healthy surplus of funds which can be used for expansion. TYM has a substantial unspent balance of more than US$97,000 from its current operations. About US$15,000 of this is thought to be required to bring the Soc San Branch to viability over the next year. The balance would be available for opening new branches. In addition, US$23,000 has been received from the Catholic Relief Service. Funding for opening new branches has been agreed in principle from CIDSE in the amount of US$60,000 and Oxfam America for US$40,000. In total this should be enough for the proposed two new branches which are projected to require about US$85,000 each of outside funding to full operation.

As it expands, however, TYM will have to improve its financial reporting. Currently TYM is not producing a balance sheet, and its accounts are not being externally and professionally audited.

Expansion and Institutionalization

Demand among poor women is strong

Field visits to communes being considered for TYM's expansion indicated strong demand for the Project's financial services among poor women, and also from the Women's Union officals and local-level Party leaders. The failure of many rural co-operatives and the absence of other formal financial institutions at the commune level mean that the people must depend on moneylenders for credit. This subjects them to high interest rates and leads to indebtedness which is increasingly widespread among the poor. The need for TYM's financial services, therefore, is strong.

TYM's institutional capacity is limited

TYM's institutional capacity to respond to the strong demand and need for it to expand the outreach of its financial services among the poor is limited. The major limitations are as follows:

- **Part-time management:** As most of the members of the management team have other duties for the Women's Union and are doing other work outside of office hours to increase their small incomes, they cannot take on a maximum, or even a moderate expansion mode. At best they will be able to add only two new branches over the next couple of years unless a way can be found for them to work full-time on TYM. To do even this TYM will need a full-time GB-experienced Training Manager and a full-time Monitoring Officer.

- **Minimal fieldstaff training capacity:** The lack of rigorous, practical GB-style training for the existing part-time field staff has led to a wide variation among them in terms of the quality of their work, and to the deviations from the GB model discussed above. This severely limits TYM's capacity for training additional field staff for expansion, as in GB-style training they are supposed to learn for themselves by observing and interacting with experienced field staff. A full-time Training Manager needs to be appointed to supervise the whole field staff training operation.

- **Lack of a master plan for expansion:** To date TYM has not formulated a master plan for its expansion towards financial viability for the organization itself. Such a plan is needed to determine the staff training and financial requirements. It should be prepared as a matter of priority. The existing master plan for scaling-up branches to financial viability and maximum outreach, prepared for the CASHPOR workshop on scaling up, can be the basis of the required master plan for the organization as a whole.

- **Lack of a plan for institutionalization:** There is no definite plan as to what kind of institution TYM should become. There is a general idea of transforming it into a bank for poor women; but there is no detailed action plan to bring this about. Probably it is unwise for TYM to think about becoming a bank in the near future. It needs more experience on the ground, more properly trained staff and a much bigger operation to ensure its sustainability. An adequate interim solution for its institutionalization might be to set it up as a subsidiary of the Women's Union with its own Board, full-time staff and autonomy in day-to-day operations.

- **Lack of adequate remuneration for the management team:** As TYM requires their services full-time but the members of the management team have other duties for the Women's Union, they end up doing a lot of work outside of office hours and having to spend considerable time in the field, including some nights. They are not adequately remunerated for their extra work or their outstation duties. One way of dealing with this would be for TYM to establish suitable honoraria and food/day and lodging allowances for its management team while travelling on official business.

- **Need for more management training:** Although members of the management team along with their interpreters have attended four CASHPOR management development workshops at the regional level on the subjects of targeting, credit discipline, financial control and cashflow management and planning, montoring and evaluation, these important management functions are still not being performed adequately in TYM. This probably indicates a need for refresher workshops in the basic GB skills at national or even project-level in Vietnam.

Little financial constraint is seen for expansion

Currently TYM is being approached by more donors/lenders than it needs. Given the widespread and deep poverty in Vietnam and the keen interest of international agencies and some foreign governments to be of assistance, there seems little doubt that this will continue, unless potential donors/lenders become discouraged with lack of increase in TYM's absorptive capacity. It is of critical importance, therefore, for TYM to do everything it can to increase steadily its institutional capacity. That would enable it to make a major impact on poverty in the country.

Soc San 2

TYM's experience in its first branch — and the stimulus given by Gibbons' evaluation report — resulted in some important changes in the new branch, Soc San 2, and a major thrust in the training of all TYM staff. In Soc San 2 TYM continued to work closely with the people's committee and Women's Union in the commune, but the programme was run by their own full-time staff, who were required to follow GB procedures strictly. At branch and project levels, Grameen Trust and CASHPOR provided technical assistance to set up professional systems of accounts and a systematic training programme. But if TYM was inching towards autonomy in its field operations, there was no progress towards establishing a separate institutional entity at head office. Mdm Tan, Project Director, still has other duties in the Women's Union; but Mdm Lan and Mdm Van are both full-time with the TYM project.

Soc San 2 had the advantage of considerable training input. In February 1995, Mdm Lee Thi Lan attended the CASHPOR-Grameen Trust workshop on Planning a Viable Branch in Dhaka, where she worked out a comprehensive plan for the development of Soc San 2.

By August, TYM's 11 full-time graduate staff were working in three communes in the new branch area, forming groups. In October-November, Ms Zalmah Mohsin, who had organized the training programme for AIM while it was expanding to 34 branches and was now its Finance Director, and Ms Saleha Begum, a senior officer from the Grameen Bank Training Institute, helped TYM set up a training programme for all TYM staff, where trainee output was synchronized with the expansion plan. Another outcome of this two-month assistance were two manuals on training and accounts. In the assessments which followed these training programmes the young graduates shone, outperforming most of the older cadres, even in the practicals.

CASHPOR's Technical Assistance Manager, Mr Ahasan Ullah Bhuiyan, had earlier spent a month at the Soc San 1 branch helping the staff to tighten the collection system and to prepare quarterly and annual work progress reports for evaluating staff and setting targets for expansion. In October an expert from Grameen Bank worked with the project to separate the branch and head office accounts and create a system to handle transactions between them.

In the new branch, a workshop was organized for key party, Women's Union and farmer's association staff in three communes to clarify TYM procedures and get their co-operation with the full-time staff. The branch office was set up in the poorest commune, Bac Phu, and the staff lived in its poor villages. In its first six months, the staff of Soc San 2 trained 67 groups (an average of 1.5 each per month) and 335 women became members. The training of the staff ensured more precise targeting and a new emphasis on the joint responsibility of groups and centres. The average income per capita per month of members in the branch is 27,647 Dong (US$28) and includes 55 female headed households and 22 women who are illiterate. The attendance rate at centre meetings is a commendable 96%.

The main problem of Soc San 2 is that it was without a branch manager for its first six months, so that supervision of centres and evaluation of staff is still weak. Because there is no manager, the branch is still not a separate accounting unit, so that transfer of money from branch to centre and loan funds from centre to branch continues to be a headache for all concerned.

The performance of the second branch has laid to rest many of the fears held by the project management about hiring fresh graduates. It has proven that 'outsiders', full-time staff from other areas, can be accepted in the commune and that young graduates can work effectively. Their 'prestige' lies in their function of servicing the financial needs of the poor, not in their local authority and political office. Equally, very poor women, including women on their own, can become good members and make effective use of loans.

Overall, the TYM project has resumed its growth. By March 1996 it had 2,407 members and was running neck and neck in numbers with Nirdhan Nepal. Seasonal loans had been introduced to answer the fertilizer needs of most borrowers and loans disbursed grew strongly to just over US$50,000. Most of the arrears which remained from the dropped-out members in Minh Phu had been collected and defaults stood at only 1%. A third branch was opened at Me Linh district and more full-time staff were recruited to staff it.

Decisions about the institutional shape of TYM, which would give it some autonomy within the Women's Union, are still in limbo. But in the branches it is clear that confidence has been restored and that TYM is moving towards a more professional mode of operation and more highly trained staff.

A Roof for the Rain

Ms. Nguyen Thi Tich, Group 45, Centre 4, Xuan Tang Village, in the Soc San 2 commune of Bac Phu is one of the poorest women in the commune. When we first met her, she lived in a bamboo-roofed house with uncemented bricks laid one on top of the other as walls. Her children had to sleep in the neighbours' houses whenever it rained. Her husband is weak but still had to work for food.

Mrs Nguyen has three children. Although they are all too young for labour only one 11-year-old child can go to school. Mrs Nguyen received a loan on October 29 1995. With the loan, she redeemed a 360 sq.m. plot of paddy land that she had been forced to mortgage before because she was so terribly poor. She also used part of the loan to pay the full price for a piglet which a richer family had let her have on credit a month before. With the balance, she bought two additional piglets (2.5kg and 1.5kg) and five hens.

She hardly let those piglets out of her sight and cared for them like precious stones. After one month she sold the biggest one for 60,000 Dong. She used this money to buy 800 pieces of roof tiles to make a roof which would protect them during the rains. She also sold two hens at 50,000 Dong and bought a blanket for her children for the cold winter months. Her net monthly income is now 80,000 Dong and, not only are they dry and warm, but they can look towards the future with some hope.

Baby Beats the Loan

Ms. Tran Thi Vien, Group 36, Centre 10, Quang Tien Commune squats in the house of a relative, because she and her husband are so far too poor to build their own. When TYM did the poverty survey in her commune, her household's per capita income per month was only 15,000 Dong (US$1.40), and the value of her total assets was only 580,000 Dong (US$53).When she joined the group training she was already heavily pregnant. But she was determined to attend all five days of the training course and she successfully passed the test. She was approved by her group to receive the first loan. But her baby was too impatient to wait. On the day that the loan was disbursed at the commune office Mdm Vien was busy giving birth.

Some of the staff wanted the loan to be postponed. They argued that she should not have been recognized because she would be on birth leave just after she joined the centre and it may make her reluctant to attend the weekly meetings. However, her group and centre were confident in her, and the loan allocation ceremony was held just after she came back home from hospital. The couple were very moved and promised to utilize the loan properly. She was allowed birth leave for 4 weeks but after 3 weeks she started coming to the meetings. With the loan, she bought eight egg hens and pig food. She earned 40,000 Dong a week from these 8 egg hens which easily covers her repayment.

**From: Review of 6 Months Operation of TYM Fund,
Soc San II Branch to Nov. 1995**

Notes

1. Tau Yew Mai Project Status Report, August 1992 to January 1994.
2. Quoted in *Credit for the Poor*, January 1995 p.2.
3. This is distilled from interviews with trainees and discussions with head office staff.
4. Quoted in *Credit for the Poor,* April 1994, p.1.

Conclusion

THE FIRST OBJECTIVE of all the four replications in this book was to test whether the Grameen Bank model could be replicated in their different countries. The result of this test, in all four cases, is a resounding 'Yes'. Whatever their difficulties, all the projects established a field operation which implemented the 'essential Grameen'. In Vietnamese communes, in the over-populated and resource-poor *terai* of Nepal, in the highly politicized villages of West Bengal and in the climatic extremes of Andhra Pradesh, the same model was applied and made to work in each case. In all contexts field staff were able to recruit poor women, with very little leakage to the non-poor; poor women formed groups and joined into centres, through which they took loans and made weekly savings, following simple and transparent procedures. They faithfully repaid their loans weekly over one year and became eligible for another, larger loan. All projects charge interest on their loans which will eventually cover their costs — as does Grameen Bank's relatively low effective interest rate of around 10% per annum. Although two were briefly tempted to spread their energies into other services, all finally focused exclusively on providing credit and savings and did not ask their staff to take on any other functions.

This success came as no surprise to the main actors in the replication movement. As was pointed out in the Introduction to this book, the Grameen Bank, APDC and CASHPOR already knew from the experience of Project Ikhtiar in Malaysia, and other replications in the Philippines and Indonesia, that the Grameen Bank model could be replicated in a number of very different contexts. The success of the four Grameen Bank replications (GBRs) in Vietnam, India and Nepal as well, establishes for once and for all the international replicability of the Grameen Bank model. Nevertheless, some ten years after the UNDP consultant told APDC that Grameen could *not* be replicated and Project Ikhtiar should *not* be funded, there are quite a large number of people still saying replication is impossible. It is hoped that the evidence produced in this book will finally lay their doubts to rest.

The main concern of Grameen Trust, APDC and CASHPOR was whether small pilot projects could be planned and organized in such a way as to establish the capacity to scale up into financially viable institutions serving large numbers of poor women. The experience of these four Grameen Bank replications (GBRs), as documented in this study, identifies the factors necessary to transform the pilot project into a full-scale credit and savings programme — although none of the four are satisfying all of them.

Successful replication is fundamentally a result of the demand from, and potential of, poor women to invest small loans profitably and repay faithfully. Scaling up small replications, however, to the level of outreach at which they make a significant impact on poverty, and can attain financial sustainability, is a much more complex question of good management, access to training in the GB methodology (as provided to these four GBRs by Grameen Trust and CASHPOR), efficient operation in the field, adequate funding and a supportive regulatory environment.

On the question of whether the four projects studied here are able to make this transition, which was the third objective of the APDC replication programme, the answer is still uncertain. Only Nirdhan Nepal has a legal status with which it can expand its outreach without concern about violating central bank or monetary authority regulations. But even Nirdhan Nepal wants to improve its prospects by becoming a development bank. SHARE is still looking for an appropriate legal vehicle and Nirdhan West Bengal and Tau Yew Mai are still just projects of their parent organizations. Thus three of the four GBRs do not yet have a suitable legal status with which to attract the large amount of funding required to scale up their outreach to organizational financial viability.

What we attempt to do in this conclusion is an analysis of the factors which affect this expansion, to see how far each project is along the road to viability and how likely they are to achieve it. Before we do this, however, we will look at the impact of these four GBRs on their poor women clients — which was the second objective of the APDC replication programme. Then it is necessary to look at the *process* of successful replication: what are the inherent difficulties of moving a typical NGO into an organization providing GB-style financial services, the crucial importance of the right leader in this process and what were the common problems that projects faced in the field during the pilot period, and how they were overcome.

The Question of Impact

If the Grameen Bank model is replicable — and the evidence is now overwhelming that it is — then we assume that the same benefits enjoyed by its clients in Bangladesh will also accrue to the clients of GBRs. That Grameen Bank members have made great gains in income, security and in social status has been documented in several comprehensive studies.[1] The end of a two-year pilot project is too early to measure this kind of impact. There are, however, a couple of indicators that suggest that the impact has been positive and widespread in all projects. The field visits showed clearly that most of the beneficiaries are poor. The fact that the repayment in Nirdhan Nepal, SHARE and Nirdhan West Bengal has been 100% from the beginning, and that TYM's repayment rate is 99%, indicates that the impact on the income of poor households has been positive. Otherwise, how would they have managed to repay so faithfully, and why would they have done so? None of the projects takes collateral, and they have no way of forcing their beneficiaries to repay. That they do so means, first, that they must have had additional income to make the repayments and, second, that they want the next loan enough to pay up the first. Otherwise they would not have been able, or willing, to repay so faithfully.

However, actually moving a family out of the poverty group is a process which, we know from the experience of Grameen Bank borrowers, will take several years. As the realists in the Siktohan Branch of Nirdhan Nepal pointed out: 'Our life does not change overnight.' In areas like Veldurti in Andhra Pradesh, for example, where climate, landlessness, caste and gender all combine to press women deeply into poverty and powerlessness, it is not expected that only two loan cycles will move a family out of the poverty group. Amongst the poorest, women will not even be able to hold their capital intact or reinvest it. The proceeds from their first loan investment will probably be spent buying stocks of food for the season of unemployment, putting a roof on the house or buying clothes so that the children can go to school. If families are deeply indebted, which is common in rural Vietnam for example, the new income will go to paying off the moneylenders. Only when women have achieved a reasonable degree of food security and made their houses proof against rain and cold, will they begin to reinvest their capital and then their profits in assets which will generate more income — beginning the process by which they will, after several years of borrowing and saving, lift their families above the poverty line.

How far this process had gone with the four GBRs in this book, is not known with any accuracy. Only Tau Yew Mai conducted an impact evaluation study. This showed that incomes rose by around two-thirds during the two-year pilot period and more than doubled by the end of the third year. Field interviews in the other three GBRs indicate a strong feeling amongst most borrowers that their lives had improved and that they were eating more regularly and borrowing less from moneylenders. There were also clear signs in house repairs, new livestock, bicycles, pigstys and warm clothing that the women were earning more income and were putting it into improvements for the family. Factors that were slowing impact on women's income growth and welfare included a very harsh opportunity climate — like the Veldurti branch of SHARE, and deep indebtedness, as in some of the poorest households in Soc San, Vietnam. But the main factor slowing women's progress in the three GBRs in India and Nepal, was the tendency there for male relatives to appropriate the loans and for the women to have little say over how it was used or control of the additional income earned from it. It may take some years of borrowing for the women to be able to assert more control. GBR field staff can certainly accelerate this process by motivating women to use their loans themselves — but they would first have to be convinced that women's own use speeds the impact on poverty as well as on the position of the woman in her family.

Demand for Credit

The fundamental strength of all four Grameen Bank replications featured in this book, and the reason all of them succeeded in replicating the GB model, is the powerful demand for credit from poor women in their ramshackle and leaking houses in every resource-poor village in Asia. It is the particular genius of the Grameen Bank model to have found a way to get through to the lowest levels of rural society and tap into this demand. Its success is rooted in the resourcefulness of poor women and their determination to make a better life for themselves and their children. This almost primordial drive fuels the replications of the Grameen Bank model. As soon as poor women in a village are convinced that the project field assistants are sincere — that there is no hidden agenda of bondage or conversion — many come forward for training. When they get loans and begin to earn extra income, then they are powerfully motivated to keep this credit window open. So long as they are sure that there will be more loans each year, most will repay with remarkable faithfulness and they will fight to overcome any problem which threatens the life of their centre.

This discipline and determination of their poor women clients has allowed each of the four replications in this book a kind of breathing space to make mistakes while they evolve from an NGO into a specialized financial institution. Fortunately for each of them, Grameen banking is a robust system, and even quite gross management blunders have difficulty destroying it. An examination of the first two years of Nirdhan Nepal, SHARE, Nirdhan West Bengal and Tau Yew Mai suggests the conclusion that it is not the Grameen Bank model which needs a pilot period for testing. Rather it is the project management which needs the pilot test — to determine if they have the will and capacity to overcome problems, to professionalize their staff and build an institution which can service the financial needs of growing numbers of poor women.

This is far from easy. As we have seen, most projects sailed through their first year on a cloud of euphoria. They were very small. Senior staff were newly returned from trips to AIM in Malaysia and Grameen Bank in Bangladesh; they were full of enthusiasm. Although initially they were subject to what Professor Ray called 'irritating, sarcastic remarks' from the moneylenders they were supplanting, and even threats from some village leaders, as soon as they were able to establish their credibility with the families of the poor, they could form groups, start weekly centre meetings and begin to see the difference that their work made in the lives of their women clients. The longer they worked the village, the more élite resistance faded, and so their confidence was boosted by a problem overcome.

Shifting from this first-gear level, of an exciting little project with a small 'family' of highly motivated staff, to numbers of branches and a much larger staff, and laying the groundwork for a shift into the overdrive of rapid expansion, is fraught with problems for all projects. Since the Grameen Bank model is known to work and its management parts have been well described and analysed,[2] why is this transition so difficult?

The first, almost universal, reason is a mindset against fieldwork amongst most NGO leaders and their graduate staff. A typical reaction of a newly-appointed manager after several days of sweaty, dusty walking to the margins of villages where the poor live, was: 'This is not the work that a PhD does!' But intensive field supervision is crucial to the success of the Grameen Bank methodology. The quality of group formation by field staff is checked through the senior management carrying out the group recognition test, including visiting the household of each potential member. This is followed by a regular series of surprise visits to centres by management staff to check on attendance and repayment discipline, to listen to members' problems, answer their queries and visit houses to check on loan utilization. This process of knowing the clients thoroughly keeps the management on top of problems before they get out of control and enables them to make decisions which answer the clients' actual needs and concerns.

In the Grameen Bank itself these functions have been routinized. The programme officer, who occupies the level of authority between branch manager and area manager, performs the group recognition test and spends most of his time doing field supervision. The monitoring department of the Bank collects information from all levels; this information is checked independently for the Chief Executive by regular performance audits conducted by the internal audit department. In a new replication, however, all these functions must be done initially by the project leader, or his deputy if one exists, until the project is large enough to justify the appointment of a programme officer between the head office and the branch managers.

Most leaders of NGOs large enough, or ambitious enough, to take on Grameen Banking, are senior people of high status in their own societies. The fieldwork demands on them during a pilot GB replication are not at all usual and not easily accepted. Each has to learn from experience that it is not enough to issue instructions from head office, to give lectures to field staff, or even to issue detailed training manuals, and expect them to be implemented in far-flung villages.

This is the weakness of a model as decentralized as the Grameen Bank. All the real potential business takes place in scattered villages at the centre meetings, under the charge of the lowest-ranking staff — the field assistants. They are without the full-time supervision which is normal for subordinate staff in conventional financial institutions. They are not the ones sent for training in GB; they do not attend the CASHPOR workshops. But their performance is central to the success of the project. It is how well they are trained, how well rewarded and motivated and how closely supervised which determines the effectiveness and efficiency of their work.

The second set of obstacles to the transition from NGO to specialized financial institution is simply the lack of experience in finance of most NGOs. Professional-level financial management has to be built pretty much from scratch. In the process an NGO has to learn the complexity of the concept of financial sustainability and come to accept its importance. Most NGOs are cursed with a 'grant mentality', grown out of the experience of funding small projects and one-off activities from donor grants. For the poor woman borrower, however, a one-off loan does little good. The process of moving out of poverty takes several years of borrowing increasing amounts of capital, coupled with growing amounts of savings that she can draw on in emergencies. If a project runs out of money and begins to cut back or delay loans to its members, poor women generally react very rationally to protect their capital by stopping repayment. The sustainability of the client's progress — and the sustainability of the project — depends crucially on continued access to these financial services by growing numbers of women. Since the experience of earlier GB replications shows that donor fashions are fickle and donors are particularly reluctant to finance operating costs, it is essential for projects to make themselves independent of donors as soon as they can by covering their costs through earned income. The factors involved in achieving this will be discussed later in this chapter.

The Importance of Leadership

Although replications, like the Grameen Bank itself, should eventually be institutionalized so that they are independent of the character of one individual leader, there is no escaping the importance of the founder and head of a project in its early years. It takes a full-time, energetic and determined project head, with a thorough understanding of the Grameen Bank methodology, to get the field operation established on a solid foundation. That leader's planning ability and his/her stature with national policy-makers and commercial bankers shapes the form and future expansion of the project.

Both SHARE and Nirdhan Nepal had this kind of effective leadership, although Mr Udaia and Dr Pant are very different people and have opposite strengths. In Dr Pant, Nirdhan Nepal had a leader of national stature and financial expertise. His policy leadership was daring — he established seven branches within two years, a form of horizontal expansion that CASHPOR warned was dangerous. But he brought it off by making full use of the regulations he himself had helped put in place during his time in the Central Bank, which required commercial banks to lend at subsidized rates to priority sectors. Dr Pant's clout enabled him to borrow quite large sums under these regulations, while his expertise in money management enabled him to cover his expansion costs from the investment of part of these funds in higher interest-bearing deposits. Nirdhan negotiated the transition from small project dependent on funding from outside donors, to expanding credit programme with 66% of its funding locally-sourced, quickly and effectively under Dr Pant's leadership.

In terms of field supervision, however, Dr Pant's role was more indirect. For most of the pilot project he was the Deputy Governor of Nepal Rastra Bank and based in Kathmandu, one day's drive from the project site. He depended on a small, well-trained management team to handle the field operation and was not in close touch with the problems they encountered. Even when he resigned from Nepal Rastra Bank and set up a second home above the project office in Bhairahawa, his focus remained on the planning and policy aspects of Nirdhan. His project manager, Mr Devendra Raut, is an experienced commercial banker, but even he has tended to rely quite heavily on his senior branch managers to carry out the actual field supervision. This lack of involvement in the day-to-day management of the centres, and the absence of an effective monitoring system, has meant that Nirdhan Nepal has continued to experience quite serious weaknesses which endanger its rapid growth.

In Mr Udaia Kumar, SHARE has the opposite kind of leader. Young, energetic, ambitious, Udaia is a hands-on field-oriented manager who revels in contact with his borrowers and his field staff. He has travelled several times to Grameen Bank and attended every possible CASHPOR workshop. As a result, he is expert in the GB methodology and a tireless promoter of it. His field operation runs like clockwork and his books show not even a single overdue payment. Udaia is trained as an accountant and this expertise is reflected in the cash management of his branches. It is a training, however, which seems to have made him super cautious in managing the project's finances. He has taken longer to shed the 'grant mentality' of the typical NGO leader, and wasted time looking for grants and soft loans when funding was available at reasonable rates from NABARD. His reluctance to pay commercial interest rates for his operating expenses has slowed his expansion and keeps his project a long way from viability.

The leadership of Tau Yew Mai is a triumvirate. Mdm Tan, the Director, Mdm Lan, Field Manager, and Mdm Van, Accountant, share the fieldwork, which consists mainly of group recognition and loan disbursement. Mdm Lan directs the training of field staff. When you see these ladies in the field, it is clear they are quite at home in the commune and in the houses of their borrowers. At least one of them goes weekly to Soc San, often staying overnight. However, three things militate against their playing an effective enough role in field supervision. The first is the distance from their office in Hanoi to the project branches in Soc San. The second is their competing duties with other projects of the Women's Union. The third is the culture of the Women's Union hierarchy, which gives considerable leeway to each geographical level to direct their own work. Since the field work relied on Women's Union cadres in the communes, the close field supervision required in the Grameen Bank model was not accepted by the cadres and was difficult for the project leaders to apply — at least until they began hiring full-time staff in their third year. The TYM management was also hamstrung on policy issues. A cap on interest rates, for example, delays progress to viability. Although Mdm Tan is a very senior officer in the Women's Union she cannot make decisions independently, but must wait on a consensus in the central committee. By TYM's fourth year, despite having overcome many problems and achieved considerable success, no decisions had yet been made on an institutional form for future expansion.

Nirdhan West Bengal was without effective leadership for most of its pilot period and most of its weaknesses derive from that one. Its founder, Professor Ray, was unable to take executive control of the project. The project director, project manager and one of the two branch managers whom he appointed and trained, saw their jobs as a stopgap while they looked for work more suited to their qualifications. No field staff were appointed for the first seven months, and by the time they were, all but one of their supervisors were either resigned, fired or mostly absent. Under these circumstances, field supervision was minimal. In the second year Mr Sengupta, a retired banker, took on the role of project director as a voluntary task, and gradually began to grapple with the needs for staff training and work systems. Mr Sengupta is a respected man of great calibre and considerable energy. The demands of his task have by degrees absorbed all of his time, but he himself sees his role as transitional until a management team can be trained to run the project effectively.

It can be seen that two rather different sets of skills are involved in the successful replication of the Grameen Bank model — management in the field, and planning and networking in the policy and fund-raising arena. Several replications have therefore divided these functions between two individuals. This is what Professor Ray tried to do, but was disappointed in the field manager. Nirdhan Nepal was more successful in dividing functions between Dr Pant and the project manager Mr Devendra Raut. The danger here is that the policy maker in the capital almost always has primacy and decision-making power over the manager in the rural backwoods; but the locus of success or failure of a Grameen project is in the field. It is therefore perilous for the policy director to remove himself too far from what is happening in the field or to depend too much on intermediaries.

The lessons for best practice in terms of leadership are that a Grameen replication in its early years needs a full-time, hands-on, field-oriented chief executive. He or she will have a primary focus on staff training and motivation, a thorough knowledge of the poor women clients and an understanding of the GB methodology which they pass on to staff, through detailed supervision of staff work in the villages and in the branch offices. Only when the field operation is well founded and staff are fully trained and the number of members large enough can a programme officer and then area manager be appointed to supervise the field work and report to the chief executive. Then the project leader can afford to withdraw somewhat, and monitor progress through the reporting system he has put in place. All going well, this should be the time that the manager needs to concentrate his attention on planning for expansion and sourcing the large amount of on-lending and capacity-building funds which will be needed for that stage. This is when a leader with some stature and influence in his own society, as well as the credibility he has established in an efficient credit operation *en route* to viability, can build relationships with commercial or development banks, donors, and government agencies.

Operating in the Field

When we look at the major problems that these four replications faced in their pilot years, we find that certain aspects of the Grameen Bank model proved difficult for almost all of the projects to implement. The first was getting the targeting right and making sure that membership was exclusively for poor women. The 'gate' that had to be effectively manned in this process was the group recognition test. The second was to allow groups to select themselves, and to accept joint responsibility for their joint decisions. This meant training staff to be leaders, but not authority figures taking power from the centres.

The difficulty with the GB model is that it turns so many normal practices on their head. It is decentralized and participant where Asian villages are intensely hierarchical. It locates decisions in the centre, amongst the most powerless, where they usually issue from the mouth of an official. It insists that unrelated women take responsibility for each other, where poverty has eroded most obligations outside the immediate family. It assumes that women are independent economic actors where society sees them only as subordinates. All projects, in consequence, spend their early years wading upstream against accepted attitudes and authorities — not only in the village, but amongst their own staff. It is not surprising that it takes time and many mistakes before the model can be faithfully implemented, and that, as Gibbons and Sukor say from their experience at AIM, 'the worst branch is the first branch'.[3]

But since these were almost inevitable problems, whether they were overcome or not depended on how strenuously field assistants were supervised by managers familiar with the Grameen Bank methodology. It follows from what has been said in the previous section, that initially field supervision was weak in all projects, except perhaps in SHARE.

Hitting the right target

Who are the poor? All projects had to decide how to define the target group, and, as we saw in the introduction, they set quite different criteria. Nirdhan Nepal and SHARE used a fairly generous land and asset ceiling; Nirdhan's cutoff was 1.5 acres of land, SHARE's was 0.5 acres of irrigated paddy land or (in the infertile Kurnool District) 2 acres of dry land. Both tightened up their targeting after the experience of the first year and advice from CASHPOR, with Nirdhan bringing down its land ceiling to one acre and SHARE shifting to an income ceiling of

Rs250 (US$8) per capita per month. Nirdhan West Bengal, in practice, used the GB criteria of 0.5 acres of paddy land or assets worth no more than the cost of one acre. TYM used a rigorous income figure based on the equivalent of 5kg of rice per capita per month.

Without a statistical sample, it is impossible to say exactly how much leakage to the non-poor there is in each project. The Grameen Bank officers who interviewed a sample of borrowers in two of the three branches of Nirdhan West Bengal, estimated that only 10% of the members were outside the target group. Field observation of the other projects suggest that the most leakage to the not-so-poor took place in Nirdhan Nepal, partly because of their high land ceiling. Staff did not motivate poor women by going from house to house at the beginning and so they missed the poorest, who are generally too frightened and lacking in confidence to approach project staff themselves. An inadequate group recognition test allowed non-poor to slide in. This observation is supported by the average loan size of the Nirdhan Nepal members in the first year of borrowing, which at US$98 was almost twice that of SHARE and three times that of TYM. There was some 'political leakage' in TYM, as members of the Women's Union executive committee in the commune were able to get into the centres, although they were not 'people without buffaloes'. But field observation suggests that this was not more than 10-15%. SHARE's targeting, particularly after it lowered its income ceiling in the second year, seems to have involved minimal leakage to the not-so-poor.

Overall then, targeting, which is fundamental to the Grameen model, does seem to have been effective in three of the four projects — and to have become more effective in all of them, including Nirdhan Nepal, as project leaders responded to problems caused in the centres by non-poor women (and CASHPOR's criticisms) by tightening their criteria. Moreover, all projects are now using a more exact and cost-effective method of identifying the poor — the house index. This method, developed by AIM and adapted to the house-styles of India, Nepal and Vietnam in workshops organized by CASHPOR and Grameen Trust, takes the guesswork and looseness out of answering the question: Who are the poor?

The Grameen ethos, however, targets not just 'the poor', but insists that even the *poorest* are bankable; in fact, that the most desperate women are likely to become the best borrowers, both in repayment and in the impact their borrowing has on their household. But it is almost impossible, initially, to get any educated, middle-class staff member to believe this — until they see it with their own eyes. The very poorest women, self-deprecating, harried and hung about with children, often husbandless, do seem like hopeless cases. Staff perceptions, combined with the fact that it is much easier to recruit the middle and upper ranks of the poor — those who are not so frightened and are maybe already doing some kind of business — means that staff usually do not motivate the very poorest, or even seek them out, unless forced by their supervisors to do so.

Professor Gibbons suggested that one way to lessen the risk and make it easier for the very poor to enter the savings and credit programme would be initially to extend livestock loans to them. These would involve allowing them to select from the local livestock market a 6-month-old female animal and requiring only that they return to the project two 6-month-old animals of the project's choice over the subsequent two years. Such borrowers would attend weekly centre meetings and make their compulsory savings, but they would not have to make weekly cash loan repayments. Later on, when their domestic economy had become stabilized, they could enter the general loan scheme.

Recognizing — or failing — the group

Nowhere was the weakness in field supervision more apparent than in the group recognition test. This is the most important quality control barrier groups must cross to get into centres and become eligible for loans. It involves a senior manager questioning each member to ensure they understand the rules and obligations of membership, and that they know each other well, and then visiting their houses to make sure that they qualify to enter. Correct targeting and the development of group responsibility and centre discipline all rest on the quality of the group recognition test.

Nirdhan Nepal is an example of poor GRT, but is by no means alone. In Nirdhan Nepal branch staff live together as a 'family' in the branch office and the seven branches compete with each other in the number of groups they can form. It is almost impossible in this atmosphere for a branch manager to fail a group that one of his staff has spent the last several weeks motivating and training. It is therefore essential for the GRT to be done by an officer senior to the branch manager. Where a programme is too small for a programme officer or an area manager to be appointed, the GRT must be done by the project manager or his deputy travelling to the branch from head office, often a considerable distance. Branch managers in Nirdhan Nepal did do GRT, although there is no data on how often this happened, and the GRT tester seldom visited the houses of members.

The GB team reported that group training in Nirdhan West Bengal was inadequate and few members understood their roles or knew the 10 Decisions, which form their social development programme. Field-shy managers in the first year meant that some groups were trained by 'facilitators' and there is no record of whether they passed a GRT or not. Later, the General Secretary of SARS did many of the GRTs, but since the three branches are 150km and 200km from the head office in Calcutta, GRT was still done sometimes by the branch managers.

Locating responsibility in the centre

The other impulse more than likely to surface without strict field supervision, is that staff, meeting targets for group formation, will form groups themselves rather than encourage women to form their own. Such staff are also likely to direct the centres rather than require centre members to make decisions and solve problems in their groups.

The prime example of this kind of top-down management was Tau Yew Mai at the time that it relied on part-time cadres as field assistants. They simply sat with the party committee and drew up a list of the poor in the commune, excluding those who were unreliable or 'too poor to repay', called them for training *en masse*, instructed them to form groups of five, and then passed them *en masse* at a ceremony attended by the political leaders of the commune. The cadres enforced repayment through their political clout rather than through group and centre accountability and the centre meeting was shorn of any real function — a fact reflected in poor attendance.

TYM paid the price for this kind of management with the collapse of several centres and resolved to emphasize the self-selection of groups and collective responsibility in their new branches. But in the absence of branch managers to enforce this policy change in the actual conduct of centre meetings, and in a commune culture of coercive control, it is realistic to expect change to be slow and incomplete.

Although TYM is the most extreme case of administered centres, it is not the only one. One indicator of how 'democratic' is the organization of centres is whether new centre chiefs and group chairpersons are elected each year. This practice, compulsory in the Grameen model, prevents a few strong women taking control of the centres. Field staff who 'direct' their centres usually work hand-in-glove with the centre chief and do not like this alliance to be disrupted. It is notable that the only project to routinely change all leadership positions annually during the project period was SHARE.

Building a Professional Operation

All four projects grappled with these problems — and with a general lack of financial expertise amongst their staff. Two of them managed to build a credible field operation and a staff equipped with the professional skills of Grameen Banking by the end of the two-year pilot project. TYM spent its second year in crisis, but had restructured its operations by the end of its third year. Nirdhan West Bengal is still in the process of upgrading staff performance and training.

With all projects this building of professionalism involved improving field supervision by management staff, tightening targeting, and setting up systems of cash control which involved giving more authority to the centre chiefs. Staff training was made more systematic; with most projects, work targets were put in place to use staff to their full capacity and staff were motivated to regard their work as a long-term career by improving their salaries.

Both Nirdhan Nepal and SHARE tightened their criteria for membership in their second year, shifting from a land ceiling to a much more tightly targeted per capita monthly income figure of Nepalese Rs280 (US$6) and Indian Rs250 (US$8) respectively. Nirdhan Nepal insisted that its staff begin work in new villages by motivating the poor from house to house. This was a training process in itself as staff realized there were many more poor 'hidden' on the fringes who never came forward at the public meetings by which Nirdhan announced its arrival in the village.

Nirdhan Nepal did not lack financial expertise; many of its management staff were ex-employees of development banks. But for the first stage of the project they were like bankers on holiday — running an operation based on mutual trust amongst the staff rather than on proper financial checks and balances. By the end of the pilot period, however, they had put in place professional methods of cash control which involved centre chiefs and group chairpersons in checking the collection sheets and a division of responsibility at the branch. They also introduced an insurance scheme to cover the death of animals bought with Nirdhan loans which lessened the risk of project failure to borrowers.

Nirdhan Nepal had the largest staff (28) by the end of the pilot period and upgraded their salaries to a level equivalent to government banks. They were left behind again, however, when a government pay revision took place in 1994. Their average monthly salary of only US$35 still seemed too low to encourage staff to reach full productivity. SHARE paid particular attention to training and rewarding its staff and in 1995 was paying an average monthly salary of US$71. SHARE's staff ran a model project in the field, with very few problems in the centres and not a single dropped payment during its first two years. Only the lack of operating funds prevented this well-motivated staff from working to full capacity and offering their services to more members.

TYM in Vietnam is the most vivid example of the common GBR pattern of a honeymoon period, followed by crisis, which forced a policy rethink and a restructuring which laid the basis for ongoing expansion. The collapse of several centres in its second year, the defection of one key cadre and the dishonesty of another, caused membership growth to stop and raised serious doubts in its management. However, demand for the programme was so strong and its members were making such good use of its loans, that it was impossible to abandon them. In the reappraisal that followed, important policy changes made possible a full-time staff and a more autonomous kind of operation. The management committed itself to a more Grameen-style emphasis on the self-selection of groups and a mutual accountability within the groups and centres, although it was recognized that achieving this within the commune context would not be easy. This policy revamp was followed by an intensive investment in staff training and in systematizing work plans and accounts at the branch level. As a result, by 1996, TYM was confidently expanding and recruiting more staff.

These three GBRs all faced up to their problems within the pilot phase when their funding was secured and they could concentrate on building an effective field operation and on training the staff they would need for expansion. Nirdhan and SHARE by their second year, and TYM by their third, had built a foundation in established branches and experienced management and field staff with which to scale up to a much larger organization. Only Nirdhan West Bengal missed this opportunity. It is only now, after the pilot phase is over, that it is grappling with its operational weaknesses and trying to put in place a training system and adequate salary scheme for its field staff. Because it is doing so at a time when it is perilously short of funds, it is working against more obstacles than it would have faced earlier.

Nirdhan West Bengal cannot be written off, however. It has recruited nearly 1,000 women into its programme; its targeting is good and the demand for its services — and the need for them in the desperately poor villages of West Bengal — is very strong. Its members believe that Nirdhan will continue to give them loans, otherwise they would long ago have stopped repaying. It is up to the management to justify their client's faith by raising the interim funding which would allow Nirdhan to build its human resources. On that foundation, it could attract the support it will need to scale up into a full-scale financial institution.

Potential for Poverty-Reduction and Sustainability

The third phase of the Grameen Bank replication programme was founded on the belief that GBRs could make a major impact on poverty in their countries if they built into their pilot phase the planning and human capacity to scale up to financial viability. This depended on their outreach, training capacity and institutional form. It meant minimizing costs through efficient use of staff while paying them well enough to keep them productive, and charging an appropriate interest rate. Finally, the GBR had to mobilize the funds required after the pilot period — for on-lending to at least 15,000 borrowers and to cover the operating shortfall required to bring at least six branches to full self-sufficiency.

Expansion of outreach and provision of financial services

It is only by expanding substantially their outreach to the poor, particularly poor women, and by providing them with the financial services that they need to pull themselves out of poverty, that the GBRs could significantly reduce poverty in their countries. All four GBRs say that this is their intention. However, not all have the same, or even sufficient, institutional capacity for doing so.

The critical path to expansion of outreach to the poor is recruiting and training the required additional field, supervisory and support staff. Three of the four GBRs had already recruited trainee staff for expansion by the time of the end-of-project evaluation: TYM had 11 trainees, Nirdhan Nepal 10, and SHARE eight. Moreover, all four GBRs work in a context in which there are large numbers of school and university-leavers competing for a relatively small number of suitable jobs. So none of them should have any difficulty in recruiting qualified trainees. Giving them adequate GB-style basic training, however, will depend on the training capacity of the GBR and on the availability of funds to pay the salaries or allowances of the trainees until they can pay for themselves by the interest income they earn.

The training capacity of a GBR depends primarily upon the number of experienced field assistants that it has, because the trainees learn by following such field assistants. Only one trainee at a time can be attached to an experienced field assistant. Sometimes the number of branches that a GBR has is used as a crude indicator of its training capacity, assuming that there are from 4 to 6 experienced field assistants in a branch. Among the four GBRs under study here, Nirdhan Nepal has (according to this measure) the largest fieldstaff training capacity in terms of numbers of branches, at five, compared to three for Nirdhan, West Bengal, and two each for SHARE and TYM, Vietnam.

In these results, however, we see the crudeness of the measure. It is true that Nirdhan Nepal had the greatest fieldstaff training capacity, with 26 field staff. But SHARE, although having one less branch than Nirdhan West Bengal, in fact had more experienced field staff, at 15, than Nirdhan West Bengal and, therefore, more training capacity. As we have seen, Nirdhan West Bengal was late in recruiting and training its field staff, relying on local 'volunteers' initially. Even by the end-of-project evaluation it still had only 11 field staff, most of them fairly new, distributed over three branches, giving an average of less than four per branch. TYM, Vietnam, had relied mainly on part-time field staff from among the Exco members of the Women's Union in the respective communes. The trainees, mentioned above, were TYM's first full-time fieldstaff. Its training capacity, therefore, was the lowest among the four GBRs.

In terms of funds in hand for staff training, TYM Vietnam was the most well-endowed, with donors almost falling over each other offering to fund their expansion. Nirdhan Nepal was in second place, but only because of Dr. Pant's clever mobilization of low interest priority lending funds from banks and depositing them at higher interest. In this way, he was able to fund field staff training from the differential interest earned and to get around restrictions on the use of on-lending funds to finance operations. In addition, Nirdhan Nepal is at the time of writing (July 1996) in the process of negotiating funding for additional branches, which will include the costs of field staff training, with USAID. SHARE, Hyderabad, has faced a chronic shortage of funds for field staff training, despite the determined efforts of Mr Udaia Kumar at fund mobilization from donors, and as a result has not been able to take full advantage of subsidized funds for on-lending available from NABARD. Therefore its rate of expansion of outreach to the poor has been lower than that of Nirdhan Nepal and TYM. At the time of writing, however, SHARE is negotiating a six-branch expansion plan with the Scheduled Caste Cooperative Finance Corporation of Andhra Pradesh, which would include the costs of fieldstaff training.

Funding was such a concern to all GBRs in Asia, including the four projects which form the subject of this book, that in February 1995, a seminal workshop took place in Dhaka on *Scaling Up to Branch Viability*. The strategy of CASHPOR and the Grameen Trust, who jointly organized the workshop, was that if a GBR could create one viable branch, it could demonstrate its ability to create others in due course — and get donors to fund this expansion. The Directors of all projects except Nirdhan West Bengal attended this workshop, which came at the end of their two-year pilot phase. They worked out individual project plans to expand one branch to break-even point.

This workshop coincided with a change of policy by the Grameen Trust to fund selected branches as a package to viability, rather than funding two-year 'pilot projects', which could leave projects stranded long before they become independent. After this workshop, GT committed funds to bring one branch in SHARE and one in Nirdhan Nepal to viability. As of early 1996, both of these Grameen Trust-funded branches were near viability — but both GBRs were complaining that this success did not seem to have made donors any more eager to fund the operating costs of bringing other branches to the same level.

However, in mid-1996, the Consultative Group for Assisting the Poorest (CGAP) of the World Bank agreed in principle, subject to project appraisal, to provide 'booster funds' for SHARE and Nirdhan Nepal to cover their projected deficits to the point of organizational financial self-sufficiency, by expanding to six branches and eight branches respectively.

Nirdhan West Bengal is unique in being the only one of the four GBRs not to have obtained funding from any source other than its original donors, APDC and Grameen Trust. Although it has husbanded these funds very carefully, in fact to the self-defeating point of failing to invest adequately in field staff training and remuneration, its reserves are now largely gone, and Nirdhan West Bengal is without funding for expansion.

Diversification of financial service portfolios in accordance with the needs of poor households has been slow among the four GBRs, especially in terms of savings products. Only Nirdhan Nepal actively mobilizes voluntary savings from its members. The other three GBRs have confined themselves to the GB-type compulsory savings and loan deduction to the group fund.

Nirdhan Nepal is also the leader in terms of diversification of loan portfolio, having seasonal and tube-well as well as general loans. TYM has introduced seasonal loans recently, and SHARE has added a limited number of housing loans. Only Nirdhan West Bengal has not added anything to its portfolio in addition to the general loan. All four GBRs could benefit from institutional capacity-building directed at financial service product development through market research.

Institutionalization and regulation

Only Nirdhan Nepal has a firm legal basis for its provision of financial services to the poor, being licensed by the Rastra Bank to do 'limited banking'. Nevertheless, its status as an NGO without equity limits its ability to perform as a financial institution. Banks are reluctant to lend large amounts because of Nirdhan's lack of equity and assets, and there is inadequate protection for depositors. Because of these limitations, Nirdhan Nepal is planning to become a Development Bank under new legislation in Nepal.

The legal situation of the other three GBRs is much less satisfactory than Nirdhan Nepal's, particularly considering the requirements for expansion and institutionalization. SHARE remains registered under the Societies Act and as such cannot attract funding from banks. It also feels uneasy about taking deposits from members, who also might get worried about the security of their savings. Recently SHARE has begun taking steps to register itself as a Non-Bank Financial Company which would be much more suitable for its expansion and institutionalization. TYM and Nirdhan West Bengal have even more tenuous legal existences as mere 'projects' of other institutions, the Vietnamese Women's Union and the South Asia Research Society, respectively. Certainly banks will not fund such operations and depositors may become reluctant for them to hold their savings. They are interim identities until a more suitable legal vehicle can be found. Most likely this will have to be done before the large amounts of funds required for scaling-up to reach large numbers of poor women become available. In Vietnam, which is still in the process of conversion to a market-oriented economy and in which banking laws are undergoing consequent changes, it is not yet clear what legal identity would be most suitable for TYM.

Another important issue concerning regulation of microfinance institutions (MFIs) dealing with the poor is that of setting maximum interest rates on loans by government and monetary authorities. As microfinance institutions dealing with the poor collect tiny amounts of savings and disburse very small loans, their unit costs are higher than financial institutions that do not deal in microfinance. Secondly, as microfinance institutions dealing with the poor provide their services in the villages of their clients this adds to the operating costs of the MFI. Hence their costs are higher than financial institutions not dealing in microfinance. Maximum interest rates set on the loans of the latter may not be sufficient to cover the additional operating expenses of MFIs dealing with the poor. Hence putting an official cap on interest rates can deny an MFI the prospect of becoming institutionally financially self-sufficient and self-sustaining — thus denying the poor the financial services they need.

In South and East Asia there is a tradition of government setting maximum interest rates on loans. Deregulation of banking has not gone far in most of these countries, as it has in most parts of Southeast Asia. Currently all four of the GBRs under study have to be concerned about keeping their interest rates to borrowers low, even though interest rate caps are not yet applied to them because of their small scale of operation and informal legal position. Interest rates are a politically sensitive issue throughout South and East Asia. Nevertheless, two of the four GBRs have managed to increase their effective interest rates essentially by switching to flat rates. Nirdhan Nepal switched from 20% p.a. interest on a declining balance basis to 20% p.a. flat calculated on the principal amount. And it changed its method of collection of interest from the 51st and 52nd week (i.e., at the end of the loan period as in GB formerly) to weekly throughout the loan period. The combined effect of these two changes was to increase NN's effective interest rate to more than 40% p.a. Similarly SHARE increased its nominal interest rate to borrowers from 10% flat p.a. to 15% flat and continued to collect interest along with repayment of principal weekly, thereby increasing its effective rate to over 30% p.a.

In neither case was there any significant backlash from existing borrowers or drop in demand from the poor for NN's and SHARE's financial services. Perhaps we can conclude from this that despite interest rates on loans being a sensitive political issue in South Asia, there is still sufficient room for manoeuvre so that MFIs dealing with the poor will be able to charge effective rates of interest sufficient for them to become financially sustainable. Nirdhan West Bengal should be able to follow the example of SHARE, although it has not yet shown any intention of doing so. Its interest rate to borrowers remains 16% p.a. on a declining balance basis, yielding the same amount p.a. effectively. This is not enough for them to become financially sustainable.

Tau Yew Mai Vietnam is charging borrowers 1.8% per month on a declining balance basis, which is the same as allowed by government for banks but is lower than the maximum rate of 2.2% per month allowed for co-operatives Presumably TYM could increase to the level of co-operatives, but it has not shown any inclination to do so. Even then, however, its effective rate p.a. would still be too low for it to become financially sustainable in the near term.

The issue of regulation of microfinance institutions working with the poor in Asia is a new one that requires careful study and deliberation. On the one hand too much regulation by central monetary authorities too soon, for example unrealistially low caps on interest rates to borrowers, might kill off the increasing numbers of private initiatives to meet the apparently huge demand for financial services among the poor. On the other hand, the rights of depositors, in particular, must be adequately protected. Already there is at least one reasonably large microfinance institution in Asia that does not allow *any* access to compulsory savings until a member leaves the programme!

It is to be hoped that self-regulation will come about through such activities as private joint deposit guarantee schemes, and the formation of national networks (guilds) of microfinance institutions working with the poor. There is one mitigating factor, however, and that is that in practice most depositors among the poor are also at the same time borrowers from the organization that holds their deposits. At most times the amounts of outstanding loans will exceed those of savings. Hence if a borrower becomes worried about the security of her savings, she can always stop loan repayment, or deduct her savings from the amount she repays. As most microfinance institutions dealing with the poor do not take physical collateral from them, there would be nothing they could do in such a situation.

Institutional Financial Viability

Even if microfinance institutions dealing with the poor expand their outreach considerably they will not make much impact on poverty unless the MFIs themselves become financially sustainable. Essentially this is because a poor women cannot pull her household out of poverty with only one or two loans and a small amount of savings. Perhaps five or six or more loans over the same number of years and substantial savings built up over that time will be required. An MFI which has not become financially viable is unlikely to exist for five years in this day and age. If it did not become financially viable and became insolvent it may well be unable to honour the savings deposits of its members, as well as leaving them without a credit line, when it collapsed. Poor households that have been struggling to lift themselves out of poverty with the help of the MFI might fall back into that morass when it withdraws. This nightmare scenario could easily happen if MFI management does not recognize the vital importance of becoming financially sustainable as quickly as possible, and take the necessary steps, including setting appropriate interest rates on members' savings and loans.

• *Setting appropriate interest rates*

We have seen above that out of the four GBRs under study only Nirdhan Nepal and SHARE have effective interest rates on loans to borrowers that are sufficient for institutional financial self-sufficiency and sustainability. There appears to be no reason why Nirdhan West Bengal cannot follow their example. Tau Yew Mai Vietnam, however, may well encounter government opposition if it attempts to set an appropriate interest rate on loans to borrowers. Further deregulation of banking may have to take place in Vietnam before MFIs dealing with the poor will have a chance of becoming financially sustainable and, hence, of making a significant impact on poverty in that very poor country.

• *Externally audited accounts and published financial statements*

It is important for regulators, donors, banks and potential investors to be able to carry out their own institutional financial analysis of MFIs dealing with the poor. This is possible only if the accounts of such MFIs are externally audited by professionally-qualified persons, and published so that any interested party can get access to them. Of the four GBRs under study here, only Nirdhan Nepal and SHARE are fully meeting these requirements. Nirdhan West Bengal has an externally audited financial statement, but no balance sheet; TYM has neither.

• *Minimizing costs*

Keeping operating and financial costs to a minimum, i.e., being efficient, is a way of hastening the attainment of organizational financial self-sufficiency. It is a way also of keeping interest rates to borrowers to a minimum.

MFIs dealing with the poor should aim to bring their costs down to the equivalent of less than 20 cents per dollar outstanding, although it will take them at least three or four years to reach the level of operation at which economies of scale make this possible. It is not expected that any of the four GBRs could achieve anything close to this in the two years of the pilot phase. As of the time of the end-of-project evaluations (approximately two years after start-up) the costs per unit of currency disbursed of the four GBRs varied considerably: from a high of 0.81 for SHARE to 0.40 for Nirdhan West Bengal to 0.43 for Tau Yew Mai to a low of 0.21 for Nirdhan Nepal. While these figures are not strictly comparable because of being taken at somewhat different ages of the GBRs concerned and ignoring any relevant contextual differences, the order of magnitude of the variation is disturbing.

Figure C.1 shows a preliminary comparative financial analysis of the four projects using a much more strenuous measure of health and efficiency than cost per unit of currency disbursed. This measures operating costs as a ratio of average loans outstanding — that is, the average amount actually out in the hands of the borrowers during one year measured against the cost of providing that service during the year. The comparison is 'preliminary' because only the figures for SHARE and Nirdhan Nepal are drawn from externally audited financial statements. Most of those for Nirdhan West Bengal and all from TYM are from project reports which have not been subject to external auditing. In any case, the comparison is subject to widely differing conditions between Vietnam and South Asia, which could make conclusions drawn for TYM invalid.

A look at this table shows wide differences in operating expenses among the projects. The lowest expenditure is Nirdhan West Bengal, because of hidden subsidies, like the voluntary work of the Secretary General and underpayment of its field staff. Tau Yew Mai also has considerable hidden subsidies in its operations, like the salaries and travel allowances of the supervisory staff from VWU, Hanoi, and the part-time services of the commune cadres who are paid only small allowances. Nirdhan Nepal and SHARE have similarly high levels of expenditure, since both were investing heavily in staff training and had salaried, professional managers and support staff in their head offices. Nirdhan Nepal's average salary levels, at US$35 per month, are much lower than SHARE's, at US$71 per month, which reflects the different salary levels in Nepal and India. However, Nirdhan Nepal had a larger staff than SHARE by the end of its second year (28 staff against 19 for SHARE) and Nirdhan was also operating seven branches compared to two for SHARE. As a result, while SHARE's operating expenses are somewhat higher than Nirdhan Nepal's, Nirdhan had a greater capacity for disbursing loans.

Consequently, where SHARE and Nirdhan Nepal differ radically is in the amount of loans their staff had got out into the hands of the borrowers. Nirdhan Nepal had average loans outstanding in its second year of more than $79,000 compared to only $15,000 for SHARE. As a result, SHARE's cost, on this measure, is an unsustainable $2.20 for each dollar outstanding compared to 40 cents for Nirdhan Nepal.

However, by the end of fiscal year 95/96, its third year of operation, SHARE had brought its cost down to $0.92 — still high, but much better than before. Nirdhan Nepal was still well ahead of SHARE in its third year in average loans outstanding and its operating cost ratio had come down to 33 cents.

Despite its low expenditure, Nirdhan West Bengal's operating cost ratio is 85 cents. Probably it is NWB's very low scale of operation, only 853 active

Figure C.1: Preliminary Institutional Financial Analysis				
	TYM	**NWB**	**NN**	**SHARE**
YEAR	5/94 - 6/95	4/94 - 3/95 **4/95 - 11/95**	7/94 - 7/95 **7/95 - 7/96**	4/94 - 3/95 **4/95 - 3/96**
Age of Project	2+ years	2 years **2 1/2 years**	2 years **3 years**	2 years **3 years**
Operating Expenses[1]	$16,590	$7,970 **$10,700**	$31,568 **$45,682**	$33,447 **$41,963**
Average Loans Outstanding[2]	$36,326	$9,391 **$17,610**	$79,125 **$139,682**	$15,213 **$45,513**
Operating Cost Ratio[3]	0.46	0.85 **0.61**	0.40 **0.33**	2.20 **0.92**
Return on Lending[4]	n.a.	0.15 **0.20**	0.05 **0.15**	0.360 **0.187**
Operational Self-sufficiency[5]	n.a.	0.17	0.10 **0.29**	0.18 **0.20**

1. Excluding depreciation.
2. Loans outstanding beginning of the year plus loans outstanding at the end/2.
3. Operating cost (excluding depreciation)/Average loans outstanding.
4. Financial income/Average loans outstanding.
5. Financial income/[Cost of funds+Operating costs(excluding depreciation)+Loan Loss Provision].

members, and their inefficient spread over three branches (giving an average of only 284 per branch) which accounts for its high unit costs. TYM's relatively low figure indicates a good potential for institutional financial self-sufficiency, despite the subsidy element.

Only Nirdhan Nepal can be said to be on track for the attainment of full institutional financial self-sufficiency, as far as costs are concerned. Although only 10% self-sufficient in its second year, by the end of its third year its income covered nearly 30% of its costs. This is even more admirable when we remember that it has the least proportion of funds from donors in the form of grants. It could be that Nirdhan Nepal's need to become self-reliant has caused it to be more concerned about minimizing costs.

Significantly NN is also the only one of the four GBRs to have actively sought voluntary savings from its members, in addition to the standard compulsory savings and loan deduction of the Grameen Bank model. As NN pays only 8% p.a. on savings deposits but 6% for subsidized priority loan funds, member savings are a relatively cheap source of funds of which it is taking full advantage. NN's savings mobilized made up 13 of its total loans outstanding at the time of the end-of-project evaluation. None of the other three GBRs were using mobilized savings as a source of funds, but rather depositing them in banks for security and income. A change of government policy will be required before they can utilize member savings to minimize their financial costs, as NN is doing.

Institutional/programme financial self-sufficiency

As of the end-of-project evaluations none of the GBRs were, of course, anywhere near institutional/programme financial self-sufficiency. Even leaving aside subsidies on the cost of funds and depletion of funds by inflation, the four GBRs were still covering only a small proportion of their costs from their interest income earned from borrowers. As they were on average only two years old they could not be expected to have become financially self-sufficient. Nevertheless, although all four GBRs had experienced an increase in their degree of financial self-sufficiency from year 1 to year 2, the gap between their current status and full financial self-sufficiency was wide indeed.

Figure C.1 shows return on lending, which is the financial income earned by each project on clients' loans and savings, over average loans outstanding. TYM is not considered since the Women's Union was not able to produce a separate set of accounts for the project.

The figures show that in Financial Year 94/95, SHARE was able to get 40 cents income from every average dollar outstanding, but there must be an error in the income figures as their interest rate of 10% flat per annum could not have generated that much income. The figure of 18.7% for FY95/96 looks more credible, as their interest rate was increased to 15% flat per annum during that year. Nirdhan Nepal's poor showing of only five cents return on every dollar out to borrowers is also misleading, however. During its second year NN was collecting interest in two lump payments at the end of the loan period. As a result, almost all the income from the larger second cycle loans was not yet *in* for the time period of this calculation.

As expected, the degree of operational self-sufficiency is low for all projects, but lowest for Nirdhan Nepal, because of its method of collecting interest on its loans. The main problems here were not only the high start-up costs (mainly for field staff training) and the slow initial rate of expansion of outreach (as group formation is in the hands of the potential borrowers), but also the impossibility of one or even a few branches covering head office costs as well as their own. A set of figures for the *third* year of operations for all projects would probably show considerable progress. The third year figures for Nirdhan Nepal, in particular, show marked progress in year three.

The strategy adopted by Grameen Trust and CASHPOR in 1995 was for each project to establish a financially self-sufficient branch as a step in the direction of institutional/programme financial self-sufficiency. But how many financially self-sufficient branches are needed for full financial self-sufficiency?

Master Plan for Institutional Financial Self-sufficiency

As of the end-of-project evaluations none of the four GBRs had a master plan for the attainment of institutional financial self-sufficiency. Their expansion, therefore, was not being guided by the requirements of attaining institutional financial self-sufficiency as soon as possible. Nirdhan Nepal and SHARE, with the assistance of CASHPOR Inc. had made plans for the attainment of a financially viable branch and were being funded by the Grameen Trust toward that goal. Since then, both NN, SHARE and TYM have tried to formulate the required master plan but none has fully succeeded. CASHPOR is trying to assist them; but its own capacity for institutional financial analysis needs to be strengthened. Clearly this is one of the main institutional capacity-building needs of GBRs and their networks in the Asian region.

Fund Mobilization

The funds required for GBRs to scale-up their outreach to large numbers of poor, and at the same time to attain institutional financial sustainability are large. To reach and service the financial needs of the 15,000 poor households that would be required for full institutional/programme financial self-sufficiency (assuming six branches from a zero starting point) probably would cost around US$1.3 million at current prices for both net on-lending funds and operating deficits to the point of break-even, according to CASHPOR's modelling. Bringing the four GBRs to full institutional financial self-sufficiency would, therefore, cost something less than US$4 million, given their progress so far. From where could such a large amount of funds come for these relatively small and unknown MFIs?

Perhaps about half of on-lending funds could come from member savings. Priority lending programmes of the various governments concerned might supply the balance, provided the rest of the GBRs could find a legal way, like NN, of receiving such funds. Gradually some commercial banks should become interested in supplying on-lending funds at market rates to GBRs that can show they are approaching financial sustainability.

The difficult problem appears to be how to cover the deficits in income as compared to operating costs until the point (probably at least two to four years away, depending on the GBR) of financial breakeven for each GBR. On average about US$250,000 would be required for each of the four GBRs for this purpose. It could be sought from governments and/or donors as grants and/or soft loans.

As mentioned earlier, CGAP World Bank has agreed in principle to provide the "booster funds" required to finance the deficits of Nirdhan Nepal and SHARE to the point of institutional financial self-sufficiency (for 8 branches and 6 branches respectively plus the head offices). This experimental funding will be combined with a technical assistance package administered by CASHPOR, designed to promote project success. If this innovative approach is successful, then it may be available to the other two GBRs by the time they have made the neccessary policy changes and strengthened their institutional capacities to become eligible.

Another way would be for the national suppliers of on-lending funds to give a four-year grace period on their repayment, and then to synchronize this repayment with expected profits after the fourth year. This would allow projects to cover most of their operating costs out of repayment from the borrowers. ADB-IFAD have come close to this in the recent loan made to the Government of the Philippines to finance the expansion and attainment of financial self-sufficiency of GBRs there. A three year grace period on repayment of principal by GBRs has been included, along with a small additional fund for building institutional capacity of branches.

All four GBRs will need to further strengthen their institutional capacities, at both field and management levels, to be able to take full advantage of the opportunities that are, and are likely to be, available to them in the foreseeable future, for scaling-up to reach large numbers of poor households while at the same time attaining organizational/programme financial self-sufficiency.

Institutional Capacity-building Needs

Expansion of outreach and service to the poor, which are essential for both poverty reduction and the attainment of institutional financial sustainability, cannot of course take place without increasing the number of trained fieldstaff. Capacity for doing this involves having both the experienced fieldstaff to do the training and the funds to pay the new trainees until the income they earn from loans disbursed is enough to cover their salaries. All four GBRs have some training capacity; but all four are short of funds to pay their trainees. Their major need, as far as training of new fieldstaff is concerned, therefore, is funding not capacity building.

Turning to management of the four GBRs, however, the need for capacity building at all levels is apparent. In Nirdhan Nepal the top management urgently needs training in effective and efficient field supervision. In SHARE, Nirdhan West Bengal and Tau Yew Mai, Vietnam the top management needs training in institutional financial analysis and management of financial institutions. The top management of all four GBRs needs training in financial modelling to organizational financial sustainability; and in the development of new financial products (new types of loans and savings) through market research. Computerization is needed to reduce work and human error in financial record keeping (especially at the branch level) and to produce timely, accurate management information, that is routinely used by top management. The top management of Nirdhan West Bengal and Tau Yew Mai needs to be made aware of the importance of accounts being externally audited and financial statements published.

Middle-level management in all four GBRs need further training in planning, monitoring and evaluation, field supervision and quality control, as well as in computerization and the development of new financial products through market research.

Branch-level management needs to be made aware of the potential of computerization in reducing paperwork and human error and in the provision of timely management information, and to be trained in the appropriate skills. In addition, its field supervision needs to be made more effective and efficient.

Most of the required management training is available at the regional level through the CASHPOR network; but it needs to be devolved to the national level, probably through the nascent national networks — to make it affordable to most GBRs.

Notes

1. For the impact of the Grameen Bank on member incomes and empowerment, see Mahbub Hossain, 1988, Rushidan Rahman, 1986, Todd, 1996, and Schuler and Hashemi, 1994. Also the World Bank study team of Khandker and others, has written as yet unpublished papers on women's status and social welfare impacts.
2. Fuglesang and Chandler, 1988; Holcombe, 1995; Bornstein, 1996; Counts, 1996.
3. Gibbons and Sukor, 1994.

Select Bibliography

Bornstein, David. 1996. *The Price of a Dream*. New York: Simon and Schuster.

Counts, Alex. 1996 *Give Us Credit*. New York: Times Books, Random House.

Credit for the Poor, Quarterly newsletter of Credit and Savings for the Hard-Core Poor (CASHPOR) Network. Seremban, Malaysia.

Dwyer, D. and Bruce, J. eds. 1988. *A Home Divided: Women and Income in the Third World*. Stanford: Stanford University Press.

Fuglesang, Andreas and Chandler, Dale. 1988. *Participation As Process — What Can We Learn From Grameen Bank Bangladesh*. Dhaka: Grameen Bank with Norwegian Ministry of Development Cooperation.

————— and —————. 1993. *Participation as Process — Process as Growth*. Dhaka: Grameen Bank.

Gedam, Ratnakar. 1995. *Poverty in India: Myth and Reality* New Delhi: Deep and Deep Publications.

Getubig, I and M. Khalid Shams. eds. *Reaching Out Effectively: Improving the Design, Management and Implementation of Poverty Alleviation Programs* Kuala Lumpur: Asian Pacific Development Center.

Getubig, I. ed. 1993. *Overcoming Poverty Through Credit*, Kuala Lumpur: Asian Pacific Development Center.

Gibbons, David S. and Sukor, Kasim. 1990. *Banking on the Rural Poor*. Kuala Lumpur: Center for Policy Research/Asian Pacific Development Center.

Gibbons, David S. ed. 1992. Revised 1994. *The Grameen Reader*. Dhaka: Grameen Bank.

Goetz, Anne-Marie and Rina Sen Gupta. 'Who Takes The Credit? Gender, Power and Control over Loan Use in Rural Credit Programmes Bangladesh.' forthcoming in *World Development*.

Harriss, Barbara. 1992. 'The Intra-Family Distribution of Hunger in South Asia.' in Sen A.K. ed., *The Political Economy of Hunger, Volume 1*. Oxford: OUP.

Holcombe, Susan. 1995. *Managing to Empower: The Grameen Bank's Experience of Poverty Alleviation*. London: Zed Books.

Hossain, Mahabub. 1988. *Credit for Alleviation of Rural Poverty: The Grameen Bank in Bangladesh*, Dhaka: International Food Policy Research Institute with Bangladesh Institute of Development Studies.

Kabeer, Naila. 1994. *Reversed Realities: Gender Hierarchies in Development Thought*. New Delhi: Kali For Women.

Kamal, Ghulam Mustafa, Mohammad Bazlur Rahman and A.R.M. Ahmedul Ghani. 1992. *Impact of Credit Program on the Reproductive Behaviour of Grameen Bank Women Beneficaries*. Dhaka: National Institute of Population Research and Training.

Khandker, Shahidur R., and others. 1995. *Grameen Bank: Performance and Sustainability.* Washington D.C.: World Bank.

Rahman, Atiur. 1986. *Consciousness-Raising Efforts of Grameen Bank.* Dhaka: Bangladesh Institute of Development Studies.

———. 1986. *Impact of Grameen Bank Intervention on the Rural Power Structure.* Dhaka: Bangladesh Institute of Development Studies.

———. 1989. *Impact of Grameen Bank on the Nutritional Status of the Rural Poor.* Dhaka: Bangladesh Institute of Development Studies.

Rahman, Rushidan I. 1986. *Impact of the Grameen Bank on the Situation of Poor Rural Women.* Dhaka: Bangladesh Institute of Development Studies.

Ray, Jayanta Kumar. 1987. *To Chase a Miracle: A Study of the Grameen Bank of Bangladesh.* Dhaka: University Press Limited.

Schuler, Sidney Ruth and Syed M. Hashemi. 1994. 'Credit Programs, Women's Empowerment and Contraceptive Use in Rural Bangladesh.' *Studies in Family Planning* Volume 25:2.

Seddon, David. 1993. *Nepal: A State of Poverty.* New Delhi: Vikas Publishing House.

Shams, M. Khalid. 1992. *Designing Effective Credit Delivery System for the Poor: The Grameen Bank Experience.* Dhaka: Grameen Bank.

Tinker, I. ed. 1990. *Persistent Inequalities: Women and World Development.* Oxford: Oxford University Press.

Todd, Helen. 1996. *Women at the Center: Grameen Bank Borrowers After One Decade* Boulder, Colorado: Westview Press.

Yunus, Muhammad. 1984 'On Reaching the Poor.' in Gibbons ed. 1994. *The Grameen Reader.* Dhaka: Grameen Bank.

———. 1991. *Grameen Bank: Experiences and Reflections.* Dhaka: Grameen Bank.

———. ed. 1987. *Jorimon and Others: Faces of Poverty.* Dhaka: University Press Ltd.